W9-AGP-379

FLYING ON THE GAGES
A Book About Instrument Flying

by

Brian M. Jacobson

Published by

Odyssey Aviation Publications
Union Lake, Michigan

Flying On The Gages
A Book About Instrument Flying

by

Brian M. Jacobson

Published by:

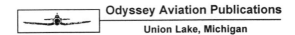 **Odyssey Aviation Publications**
Union Lake, Michigan

All rights reserved. No part of this book may be reproduced or transmitted for any reason without permission of the author, except for brief quotations for the purposes of a book review.

The author has gathered information for this book from many sources. Every attempt has been made to assure its accuracy, however, this book and its contents are sold without warranty, express or implied, of any kind, and neither the author or the publisher will be liable for any damages resulting from its use.

The aeronautical charts and graphs used in this book are for purposes of illustration only and are not to be used for navigation.

Copyright © 1996 by Brian M. Jacobson
Library of Congress Card Number: 96-69665
ISBN: 0-9653640-9-7

Edited by Rick Darby
Cover by Different By Design

Dedication

This book is dedicated to Sabbie and Louise Ludovici, two of aviation's finest who have never received the recognition they deserve.

ACKNOWLEDGMENTS

I wrote this book on my own but there are so many other people who took part in assuring its success that it is impossible to thank each and every one. But here's a partial listing.

My wife Virginia proofed the original mauscript and provide support throughout the entire project. Rod Machado provided much inspiration and knowledge that he gained while writing his wonderful books that he helped me avoid some of the pitfalls he ran into. My editor Rick Darby did a superb job as did Yvette Mortz of Different By Design, who designed the cover. Susan Lurvey from the Boeing Aeronautical Library of the EAA Aviation Foundation provided some insight into the cover design. Others who helped out behind the scenes were Leo Voglrieder Jr., John Macchia, Bob Lambert, Mark Lacagnina, Russ Lawton, Richard Taylor, and Howard Fried.

Contents

INTRODUCTION

Frank Comerford owned a flight school at Hanscom Field, a joint civil-military facility just outside Boston, Massachusetts. A designated examiner, he performed many of the flight tests conducted in eastern Massachusetts. On a perfectly clear fall day in 1971, I was knocking on Frank's door, performing the ritual of a student instrument pilot looking to upgrade my license. In hand were my application for the instrument flight test that had been endorsed by my flight instructor, the local charts and approach plates, and my venerable plastic hood (we didn't have Foggles in those days) that had nearly reached its service life. I hoped that it would not be a regular part of my flight kit after this day.

I thought that I was fully prepared for the oral. I had spent hours and hours with friends and my instructor, and by myself, pouring through books, approach plates, charts, weather information, and anything else I thought would be pertinent to the flight test. Of course, flying a rental airplane costs money, so there was no extra flight time, only the amount necessary to get me ready for the checkride. I was confident, but I had heard plenty of flight test "war stories" from people who had more experience taking checkrides.

My preparation paid off in the oral. Frank only had to "jog" my memory a couple of times, and then I knew what he wanted to hear but didn't understand what he was asking because of how he phrased his questions. He had me flight-plan to Manchester, New Hampshire, a distance of only 28 nautical miles (NM). Manchester didn't have approach radar at the time, but had an instrument landing system (ILS) and a very high frequency omnidirectional range (VOR) approach.

The airplane I was flying, N8597N, a Piper Cherokee 140 that was a lease-back to the flight school I studied at, didn't have an automatic direction finder (ADF). In those days you were not required to do all the approaches, only those that the airplane was equipped for. I didn't mind that because I had found the ADF a very difficult instrument to deal with the few times I had used one in another airplane. In fact, it wasn't until many years later that I became reasonably proficient at nondirectional beacon (NDB) approaches.

I flight-planned to Manchester, then spent an hour discussing the flight and answering Frank's questions about airspace, weather, rules, and regulations. Then he said, "Let's go fly." I was happy. I knew I had done well on the oral, and hoped I could do as well in the airplane.

I have always been nervous about checkrides.

I have always been nervous about checkrides, especially those I have had to fly with Federal Aviation Administration (FAA) inspectors. I suppose the nervousness is normal, and I've known others with the same affliction. I never figured out if it was the fear of busting the ride, or that the inspector or examiner might find out that I didn't know something that I should, that caused my unease. All the checkride war stories that I had been exposed to certainly didn't help matters either.

Frank and I climbed into the Cherokee. I was careful to use the checklist, started the engine, turned on the radios, and called ground control for my clearance to Manchester. I had spent hour upon hour listening to the control tower at Worcester, my home base, and knew I could copy the clearance without hesitation. I was cleared direct to the Manchester VOR at 4,000 feet. I didn't even have to fly an airway to get there.

The traffic in the Boston area is always heavy, and we sat at the end of Runway 29 for 10 or 15 minutes waiting for a release from Boston Approach Control. When it finally arrived the tower controller cleared me for takeoff with a right turn on course. Frank took the controls for a moment right after takeoff while I put on the hood and adjusted it. Then, back at the controls I made the right turn and headed for Manchester. Frank said little on the short trip north, but he did say he wanted me to hold on the localizer, then do an ILS approach and a VOR approach.

When Boston Departure handed me off to Manchester Approach, I gave Manchester the request, and the controller told me to intercept and hold north on the localizer, left turns, at the intersection of the Lawrence (LWR) 290 degree radial at 4,000 feet. He also gave me an expect-further-clearance time. I looked at the approach plate and tried to figure out how to enter the hold. I finally decided to use the teardrop entry because it would keep me inside the holding airspace. I was always having trouble figuring out entries to holds.

I intercepted the localizer using the number one VOR and flew it inbound. The radio was a Narco Mark 12B, a fairly common nav/com in those days. I set the number two for the Lawrence VOR and adjusted the omni-bearing selector (OBS) accordingly. It was a Genave Alpha 200 that had the VOR indicator built into the radio itself. It was not a true nav/com because you could only use one of the functions at a time.

My nerves were starting to get to me. I wasn't too sure about the hold, though I was properly lined up on the localizer. I watched the needle on the number two nav indicate that I was passing the LWR radial and began the turn into the hold. I timed the outbound leg of the teardrop carefully, started the turn back toward the localizer and intercepted the back course. I was doing fine, but was still apprehensive, maybe because Frank hadn't said anything. I even took a moment to wonder if he was sleeping. I had a flight instructor go to sleep on me while practicing turns during my early-instrument training.

The next time I looked at the number two nav I immediately became suspicious.

The next time I looked at the number two nav I immediately became suspicious. The needle was centered, even though there was no way it could be centered yet. Then I looked more closely and realized there was no to/from flag. I checked the radio to see if he had turned it off, but it was still on. I tuned the number one radio to the LWR VOR and it came up instantly. I looked at the circuit breaker for the number two to see if he had pulled that. It was in.

I didn't know what he had done, but I knew he had done something. After all, he was a wise old bird, had been around many more years than I, and probably knew how to shut the VOR off without it looking like he did it. But just to be certain, I tuned the radio to the Manchester VOR. Nothing! I checked that the radio was set for the VOR function instead of the com function. It was.

My nerves were gone instantly. I became angry at Frank. That was a cruel trick to pull. I didn't even consider that the radio had failed. Perhaps I had listened to too many checkride war stories that placed the blame for all failures and incidents on the examiner.

Now I had to stay on the localizer and hold at the Lawrence 290 degree radial using only one radio. That meant switching frequencies back and forth on the number one. I did it better than I could have imagined before the flight. I was going to show this turkey that knocking out one of my radios was not a big deal to me. One thing that helped was that the winds were light and didn't provide much interference.

We went around the pattern twice and Frank said not a word until we hit the intersection the second time around. "Okay, let's get on with the approaches," he said, then was quiet again. I called Manchester approach and told them we were ready for the ILS. The controller cleared me for the approach. I completed the procedure turn and flew the approach to minimums, although I bumbled the glide slope once or twice but got right back on it. I looked up at minimums, saw the runway, and was going to land when he told me to go around. Then I did the VOR approach with good results and another missed approach. Then Frank told me to take the hood off and fly VFR back to Hanscom Field.

On the way back to Bedford I played with the number two radio, trying to get it to work again. He watched me. Then I asked him if he had done anything. He said no. "You'll want to get it fixed, though, if you want to fly this thing in the clouds." I settled back in my seat and smiled. Now I had a real checkride war story to tell, and I was satisfied with my performance.

My misdirected anger had allowed me
to shed my nervousness and concentrate
on flying the airplane.

Frank gave me my instrument rating and told me he was impressed with my oral and with the way I handled the radio failure. I didn't tell him about my misdirected anger, which had allowed me to shed my nervousness and concentrate more on flying the airplane. I flew back to Worcester prepared to move on into the world of instrument flying.

That was my initiation into instrument flying. Everyone has their own story to tell, and in this book I will tell you about many things that have happened to me through the years. This book is not intended to be an instrument manual. Manuals are often boring and difficult to get through. Instead, I want to give you some of the basics of instrument flying plus an indication of what it is really like to fly on the gages. Some of you already have limited experience with it, but many pilots who get their instrument ratings seldom maintain their currency and proficiency. Perhaps what I have written will jog not only your memory but the excitement you once felt for instrument flying.

For those who wish to become professional pilots one day, the information contained in this book will add to your knowledge, perhaps fill in some of the blanks that your instructor left in your training. The experiences detailed in the book should provide you with valuable insights that most pilots find impossible to get without filing an IFR flight plan and flying in the clouds yourself.

CHAPTER ONE

GETTING UNDERWAY

The pace of instrument flying by the general aviation population increased dramatically during the aviation boom of the late 1960s and early 1970s, for several reasons. First, avionics manufacturers reduced the size of the "black boxes." Instead of having large, remote-mounted units in a baggage compartment or on an avionics shelf, nav/coms were installed in the center panel at the pilot's fingertips. With the reduction in size came a reduction in prices. For the first time avionics manufacturers were building gear designed for general aviation aircraft. Aircraft manufacturers offered packages of avionics that included dual nav/coms, glide slope, ADF, transponder, and three-light marker beacons. More airplanes had the equipment necessary for pilots to "fly blind."

Pilots and aircraft owners demanded more utility from their aircraft. No longer was it acceptable to cancel a business or charter flight because the weather was not VFR. As corporate flying came to prominence during that period, in large and small general aviation aircraft manufactured for that role, more and more pilots trained on instruments, got their ratings, and offered their services to the industry.

Even those who flew solely for their own pleasure determined that the benefits of having an instrument rating were significant. The training required that a pilot be more familiar with his or her aircraft and the way it flew. Flying on the gages required a smoothness of control that many VFR pilots lacked. So, when the instrument pilot flew with reference to the outside world, he or she was a better pilot.

A pilot could now fly an instrument approach instead of trying to remain clear of the clouds and terrain during the search for the field.

As in other segments of aviation, the average general aviation pilot discovered the increased utility of his or her airplane. Now a pilot could fly with confidence in or above a cloud deck instead of "scud running" below it. He or she could fly a published instrument approach that led directly to an airport or runway instead of flying only hundreds of feet off the ground while trying to remain clear of the clouds and terrain during the search for the field.

Instrument flying is not easy because man is not equipped to fly in the clouds without some artificial method of balance control. We don't realize it in our everyday lives, but our eyes are our principal source of balance. When we are in the clouds and can no longer see the ground our senses lie to us. That is because the fluid in our inner ear becomes our primary source of balance information, and it is faulty. It takes too long to catch up with reality, and by the time it does we have already changed our attitude based on misinformation.

In the early days pilots were taught to fly "by the seat of their pants." "Feel the airplane and what it is doing," flight instructors would say. And to do that pilots used their major connection to the airplane. Hence the "seat of the pants" expression. Second, they would feel the controls through the stick and rudder pedals. Instructors taught their students to disregard any instrument indications, if indeed there were any flight instruments in the panel, and rely instead on their sense of how the airplane was flying. As aviation progressed pilots were reluctant to switch to enclosed cockpits because they were afraid they would not have the same sense of their airplane in flight without the wind flowing around them.

It did not take long for the military and the burgeoning airlines of the 1920s to realize that the airplane could never reach its full potential until pilots could fly in all weather conditions, and to do that required expertise with instruments. Elmer Sperry Sr. was a pioneer in the development of aircraft instrumentation. He invented the turn and bank indicator that informed pilots if they were turning right or left. Pilots realized that if they coupled that information with changes in airspeed they could do a reasonable job of flying in the clouds, but it was too easy to become confused because there was no real attitude information. Many pilots lost their lives trying to teach themselves the art of instrument flying, usually when they got caught in weather and could not keep the airplane upright.

Jimmy Doolitte proved to the world on a foggy day in 1929 that routine instrument flying was possible.

When Sperry developed the artificial horizon and directional gyro, that changed. Now a pilot had a reference to the horizon that he could use for correct balance or attitude when he or she was in the clouds. Jimmy Doolittle did the flight testing and proved to the world on a foggy day in 1929 that routine instrument flying was possible.

That was not the end of the problem, though. A great deal of training was required before pilots could fly on the instruments with proficiency. They had to learn to read each instrument individually, interpret them collectively, create a mental picture of where the horizon was in relation to the airplane, and act on the information. And don't forget that there were more than two instruments. In addition to the artificial horizon and directional gyro, the pilot had to analyze information from the airspeed indicator, altimeter, vertical speed indicator, and turn and bank indicator. And he or she had to scan those instruments constantly. Any-

thing else that went on in the cockpit was a distraction.
Little has changed in the art of instrument flying. We still interpret the same instruments the same
way. But our ATC system has grown more complex
over the years and requires more of every pilot's attention. In addition to scanning the instruments we must
talk to ATC on the radio, perform precise navigation,
deal with system failures as they occur, think ahead of
our airplanes, and make the decisions necessary that
will ensure a safe flight. It is not an easy task for any
pilot, especially a lone pilot flying a light single or
twin without the benefit of an autopilot.
So, where does one begin his or her quest to fly
in the clouds? If you have a private pilot's license you
probably have already begun. Student pilots are taught
from the first day the relationship between the instruments and the horizon. They are encouraged to use the
instruments, the horizon, and the feel of the airplane
in unison to develop their sense of aircraft balance and
control. But don't be fooled. Just because you have a
couple of hours of basic instrument flying under your
belt, mostly flying straight and level or practicing the
life-saving 180-degree turn, chances are you will not
get very far with that little experience. Unfortunately,
too many pilots before you have proven that.

*One pilot left a lasting impression on
me because he killed my next-door
neighbor.*

One of those pilots left a lasting impression on
me because he killed my next-door neighbor many years
ago when I was a teenager. It was a Thanksgiving Day

in the early 1960s. Henry was a student in the aviation program at Parks College in St. Louis. He and several friends had flown from St. Louis, Missouri to Worcester, Massachusetts in two rented Cessna 182s for the holiday. The weather on the day of the accident started out VFR, and the pilots gave friends and family rides in the airplanes. Everyone had a good time. But late in the afternoon the weather deteriorated, and four of the Parks students, including Henry, decided on one last flight before securing the airplane for the day. They got a special VFR clearance out of the Worcester control zone and quickly became engulfed in the clouds and fog that was overspreading the area. They hit the 600-foot level of Mount Wachusett, a 2,000-foot mountain about 20 miles northeast of the Worcester Airport. The four occupants of the aircraft were killed. I clearly remember the police coming to inform Henry's parents of the accident and reading about it in the newspaper the next day. Naturally, it was front page news, as are most general aviation accidents. Let that be an early lesson to you that without an instrument rating you have no business flying in the clouds or attempting to scud run in IFR conditions.

I have always advocated that every pilot have an instrument rating, though I would not go so far as to say it should be a regulatory requirement. Flying on the gages instills a basic smoothness into one's flying that probably would take years to develop otherwise. Even if you never fly IFR after getting your rating, you will be a better VFR pilot. Some question whether the expense is worth the result. Each pilot will answer that question for himself or herself, but getting the rating is demanding and satisfying for most people, and the results are apparent in their flying.

Continuously increasing one's level of smoothness is the quest of the instrument pilot, and that usually comes with experience. Also with time and practice comes the ability to sit back and relax while you perform your duties. The more relaxed you are the better your flying will be because you will be farther ahead of your airplane. If there is a key to successful instrument flying, that is it. Having the time and brain power available to consider future events means your scan rate is fast enough to absorb what the instruments are telling you, and that you are not being overworked. An instrument pilot who is frazzled because he or she is having a hard time keeping up with events needs the help of a good instrument instructor.

Another mark of a good instrument pilot is that he or she knows what to do or where to go should anything unexpected occur to threaten the safe outcome of the flight. The required skill is called making decisions, and the earlier a pilot makes his or her decisions the better the results. By having your decisions made before anything untoward occurs you can allow yourself the luxury of concentrating on the problem at hand while flying toward your new destination. It frees brain space for use in dealing with events that demand resolution instead of being forced to divert one's attention to other matters.

A frazzled pilot gives up much of his or her authority. Events, instead of the pilot, begin controlling the situation.

Frazzled pilots have little or no brain space left

to consider alternatives when faced with a problem. Almost all of their attention is spent simply flying the aircraft. So they listen to others instead of making the decisions themselves. And others cannot make the decisions. A controller may offer a solution to a pilot, but only the pilot can judge whether it is the best for that situation or not. Other pilots flying other airplanes may advance suggestions, but deciding on the spot that something is the right thing to do only because it sounds good can lead to disaster. Without giving any course of action the proper degree of thought a pilot gives up much of his or her authority. Events, instead of the pilot, begin controlling the situation.

It is essential that any new or recent instrument pilot begin slowly. I did not do that. Fortunately my instrument instructor, Dick Franklin, a product of the military who had plenty of experience in the soup, gave me the confidence and the proper level of training to get me through my impetuous beginnings. Too many pilots are not that lucky.

Personal limits must be taken into account in ensuring one's survival in the clouds. It is not wise for a fledgling instrument pilot to seek minimums weather to build time on the gages. There is too much that can go wrong too quickly, and it's the new instrument pilot, or one who has not maintained a reasonable proficiency, who will become frazzled because his or her brain cannot handle all that can happen if anything goes wrong. Without excess brain power the pilot may continue to fly the airplane but only for so long before being overpowered by events.

Sounds difficult, doesn't it? The instrument rating is undoubtedly the hardest individual goal to reach in aviation, and harder yet to maintain. That is because flying in the clouds is serious business. But to those who play by the rules it becomes second nature, like flying VFR, or driving your automobile in heavy traffic. Decisions are easier to make, and as your experience level builds your personal limits change. On the day when you do that first approach to minimums, whether you land or make a missed approach, you will have a feeling of accomplishment because you are operating in a world meant for professional pilots, not amateurs, and you are operating competently and confidently. There are not that many amateurs in other fields who can claim that kind of success.

If you have yet to begin your instrument training the most important decision you will make is selecting your instructor. Many pilots give this little thought and begin their training with their basic instructor. If he or she is rated as a Certified Flight Instructor - Instrument (CFII) that means the FAA, or a designated examiner, has determined that they are qualified to teach instruments. But many young instructors don't have the experience behind them. Find someone who has been there and done it, who can pass along the benefit of that experience. I believe you will learn faster from an experienced instrument pilot who is also an instructor, and you will have less tendency to become a mechanical instrument pilot or one who does not develop a feel ("seat of the pants") for the airplane. Too often pilots get caught up in flying the instruments and disregard any feedback from the airplane itself. And instructors who have little instrument time are less likely to help a student develop their ability to feel how the airplane is behaving. Without a basic feel for the airplane you cannot be a smooth instrument pilot.

There is a big difference between the old seat of the pants flying and accepting or recognizing feedback from your airplane while flying on the gages. I will reiterate that you cannot fly the airplane solely by feel in the clouds because you have no reference to the natural horizon, but maintaining altitude is much easier when you can feel that the airplane is slightly out of trim and make the slight adjustment necessary without having to rely on the gages for that. The resolution of the instruments is not always good enough to give you that information, and if you should be having problems maintaining altitude it could be that you are not yet capable of fine tuning the trim because you are not correctly feeling the feedback from the airplane.

Flying on the gages is something you must do regularly if you are to remain proficient at it.

So, after you select your instrument flight instructor the work begins. Don't kid yourself. It is hard work. It will take much of your time and demand a great deal of your energy. Many pilots begin instrument training never to finish. They don't put enough effort into it to show positive results and soon tire of the project. Flying on the gages is something you must do regularly if you are to remain proficient at it, even after getting the rating, and a student instrument pilot who does not fly at least once a week will regress more than progress.

The airplane you fly when doing any kind of training is important, and I frequently have people ask me whether it makes sense to buy an airplane to learn to fly in or to rent from a fixed-base operator (FBO) or flight school. The answer is different for each person and the considerations must be weighed carefully. Many people will get their private license, then buy an airplane in which they will take their instrument training. Others jump right in from the very beginning.

There are pros and cons to owning and renting, but rare is the student or potential student pilot who has the expertise to know what kind of airplane he or she desires, never mind the correct way to go about the purchase without getting hurt physically or financially. Once the private license is in the bag the fledgling pilot is somewhat more informed about the types of airplanes that are out there, what they will do, how much they cost to operate, and which ones will meet his or her needs. If the pilot is certain that the airplane that he or she will buy has long-term ownership prospects then perhaps the purchase is justified before beginning the instrument rating. After all, taking your instrument training in the airplane that you will routinely fly afterward will save you the trouble of transitioning later on. From a financial aspect, pilots often like the idea of putting their money into something they own rather than paying it to a flight school for rental time. Nevertheless, if you intend to buy an airplane to conduct your basic or instrument flight training be very careful how you proceed.

Get professional assistance to be sure the airplane is priced right, is what you expect it is, has the equipment you need to fulfill your desires, and most important, that everything is in good operating condition. Don't rely on a salesman who has a beautiful-looking Skyplodder that was only flown by a little ol' lady on Sundays. Believe me, the salesman's pocketbook will dictate what information is passed on to you.

A poorly maintained airplane will cost you more money in the long term then renting, will lead to events in the air that you would rather not experience, and will probably not be available when you need it because it is in the shop. That will frustrate you in many ways, including the amount of money you have to sink into an airplane, and the delay in your training that probably will cause a loss of proficiency and the need to repeat many lessons.

In this chapter we have touched on some of the items we will deal with later in the book. My intent is to give you a fair amount of basic knowledge accompanied by some insights that will make your assimilation of the information easier.

So, let us get started on the way to flying on the gages.

CHAPTER TWO

INSTRUMENT SCANNING AND AIRCRAFT 'FEEL'

Instrument flying is not easy. That statement is not intended to drive you away from it, but to alert you to the work that lies ahead. If you are just starting, your lessons should be kept to an hour or less until you get used to the heavy workload. Trying to do much more than that in the beginning will tire you quickly and result in a waste of time and money.

Probably the first thing your instructor will teach you is to scan the instruments. This is the most vital part of instrument flying, and without learning how to do it well you will not fly an airplane successfully in the clouds. Scanning the gages is the basic element of any instrument curriculum, and in later stages most problems that you have will relate to how well you are scanning.

The speed at which you scan the instruments will directly affect how you interpret them and control your aircraft. But simply looking at one instrument then the next in rapid succession will do little good. You must take the time to interpret each gage as you look at it, then create a mental picture of what the airplane is doing in relation to the horizon. If you are not scanning and interpreting fast enough, aircraft control will suffer because changes in attitude can happen quicker than a rusty or inexperienced instrument pilot can scan.

Each flight instrument gives you a different part of the attitude picture and some tell you more than others. You will find it easier to rely more on the attitude indicator for pitch and bank information than to form your mental picture from scanning it and other instruments, like the altimeter, turn and bank indicator, or turn coordinator. But there are several problems with that relationship.

Relying solely on one instrument is dangerous.

First, relying solely on any one instrument is dangerous. What happens if it fails? Will you have the ability to fall back on the others? If you depend on the attitude indicator for too much information and it quits, you will wind up having to interpret just as much information from more instruments. That is called flying "partial panel" and means you will take more time to reach the same attitude conclusions - in other words, your scan will slow down. The longer it takes you to come up with the correct attitude interpretations the worse your aircraft control will be.

It is very easy for any instrument pilot to get in the habit of staring at the attitude indicator and becoming overly dependent upon it. Often instructors fail to pick up the fault because the student's flying tends to improve initially. But he or she will eventually reach a plateau beyond which it will be hard to progress. That is because the minute changes in attitude required to maintain a trimmed condition cannot be done by relying on the attitude indicator. They are the result of feedback from the aircraft's controls, or how the pilot feels the airplane, and the very slight changes in the altimeter for pitch and the directional gyro or turn and bank indicator (turn coordinator) for roll. We will skip yaw for the moment.

So, a pilot who fixates on one instrument to the exclusion of the others is neglecting some very important detail. The altimeter and airspeed indicator will show you before any other instrument that your pitch attitude is changing. That is because the resolution of the attitude indicator is not good enough to show minute changes that lead to slow changes in altitude. If the pilot focuses solely on the attitude indicator he or she will not see any altitude discrepancy until the next time the altimeter is scanned. How long might that be?

If the airplane "creeps" up or down more than 300 feet while on an instrument flight plan an altitude violation is likely to result. If the air is smooth and the rate of change is 50 feet per minute a pilot would have to stare at the attitude indicator for six minutes before reaching the critical altitude where a violation can result. That is not likely to occur. But IFR weather usually brings with it turbulence that will cause the changes to occur much faster. If the altimeter or vertical speed indicator is neglected a large altitude incursion could result.

When we fly instruments
we must seek perfection.

When we fly instruments we must seek perfection. Any altitude deviation can lead to a loss of legal separation between two airplanes at concurrent altitudes. While controllers may not get too excited about deviations until your encoding altimeter reports that you are more than 300 feet from your assigned altitude, technically you must remain at your assigned altitude with no exceptions. If you are staring at the attitude indicator to the exclusion of the other instruments and allow the airplane to creep up or down you are not doing the job that your license and instrument rating purport you are capable of doing.

Your scanning time frame depends on how quickly you scan the panel and interpret what you see. We could be talking fractions of a second or several seconds or more. That will depend on your experience level and proficiency. So you must understand that all the flight instruments are important. It is accepted practice to teach that certain instruments are primary for certain conditions, yet it is the combination of all the instruments that allow the pilot to develop the mental picture of what his or her airplane is doing in relationship to the natural horizon, and they are all just as vital to that image.

Another old argument, pitch versus power, surfaces during instrument training. It is important that you understand which power levels and pitch attitudes will create the flight conditions that you desire. In each airplane you operate, straight and level flight at a given airspeed is represented by a particular pitch attitude and engine revolutions per minute (RPM) or level of power. In straight and level flight try increasing power from cruise to normal climb power and what happens? The airplane climbs. You can keep it from climbing by decreasing the pitch attitude but then what happens? The airspeed increases.

If you are climbing at too high an airspeed what do you do to change it? Your power setting for the climb is predetermined. If your aircraft is equipped with a fixed pitch propeller you will have the throttle all the way forward, while an aircraft with a constant speed propeller uses a particular manifold pressure and RPM. If the airspeed in the climb is too high you increase back pressure, or pitch, to reduce it. If it is too slow you decrease back pressure, or pitch, to increase it.

The reason that is an issue at all is because there is so much happening in the cockpit at any given time in relationship to aircraft control around the three primary axes that people tend to muddle the issue with incorrect perceptions. In a pilot's quest for smoothness it sometimes appears that the controls may work differently, and the naysayers in the pitch versus power argument take advantage of that. If you are cleared to climb to a new altitude you will be increasing power as you add back pressure to increase pitch. Combining the two operations into one results in a smooth change from level flight to the climb attitude. But that doesn't change the basic way you maintain control of the airplane.

Cross check all the instruments. It is the only way you can tell if one of them is feeding you bad information.

Pilots can facilitate their instrument flying by learning what pitch attitudes and power settings are required for given operations. Level flight at a given airspeed will require a particular pitch attitude and power setting, and the same is true for climbing and descending. In level flight you want to adjust the miniature airplane so it is aligned with the artificial horizon and from there you can decide how many degrees of pitch up or down are required for the desired effect in the climb or descent. But don't forget to cross check all the instruments. It is the only way you can tell if one of them is feeding you bad information.

Should the attitude indicator decide to do a slow wingover and dive for the limits of its gimbals, if you are staring at it to the exclusion of the other instruments you will chase it while failing to realize that there is something very wrong. Do you find that hard to believe? Don't. There have been accidents caused by that very type of failure.

To that end a pilot's eyes must always be moving when he or she is flying in the clouds. And what we have discussed thus far only concerns the flight instruments. When you add into the equation the necessary navigation instruments and those that monitor the aircraft's systems and state of operation, the instrument pilot is a very busy body.

Instrument pilots have problems with yaw control because their scan is defective. They simply do not or cannot take the time to scan the ball in the turn and bank indicator or turn coordinator. They don't want to ignore it but they do. So, what happens? In a climb the single engine airplane is always turning to the left, and the pilot cannot understand it. Finally he or she gets tired of constantly turning back to the required heading and looks harder at the instruments until realizing that more right rudder is needed to overcome P-factor. As soon as the right rudder is applied the airplane performs better. The climb rate increases, the heading stays where the pilot wants it to, and there is no longer a need to hold right aileron to overcome the turning tendency.

As much as pilots are taught to push that right rudder in a climb, when they get into the clouds it is often forgotten, probably because they cannot see the real horizon moving any more. The directional indicator will show the left heading drift, and the attitude indicator will display a slight left bank that the pilot will continously be correcting. If the airplane is in turbulence the pilot might not even notice it, but he or she should feel that the airplane is not flying straight. If the pilot flies instruments mechanically - that is, strictly by the instrument indications with no seat of the pants feel - he or she will not realize the difference until it finally shows in the instruments. A mechanical pilot will correct for the problem with aileron and wonder why the airplane wants to turn left, while neglecting the reason for it that is depicted in the ball. Some pilots never realize how hard a long climb can be in a light single with the right foot constantly pushing on that rudder. It gets tiring. Some light singles offer a rudder trim that can assist, essentially relieving the strain on the right leg during long climbs. But don't forget to reset it once you reach your cruising altitude.

Forgetting the right rudder in a climb can be attributed to fixation on the attitude indicator and a lack of correct interpretation of all the instruments. And I reemphasize that some pilots are taught from their first basic flight lesson to put too much reliance on that instrument, and they start becoming mechanical instrument pilots long before their first instrument instruction flight.

In level flight the mechanical pilot will trim the ailerons to keep the wings level if the airplane has an aileron trim tab. But he or she will not even think of doing anything with the rudder, because the pilot doesn't look at the ball and fails to see that it needs some attention also. So the airplane is flown in an out-of-trim configuration even if it seems to go straight. Does that have an effect? Sure it does. The airplane is not as efficient when it is out of trim, so it cruises at a somewhat slower speed and may burn a little more fuel than it should for the overall trip.

If your hand, fanny, and feet are not relaxed, you will not feel any feedback.

Pilots who don't develop a feel for what the airplane is doing by using a combination of the instrument indications, the feedback they get from the seat of their pants, and their connection via hands and feet to the controls may have anxieties about the airplane's attitude and simply grasp the controls too hard. If your hand is not relaxed you will not feel any feedback in the control wheel. The same goes for your fanny and feet. Think about it. What happens when you bank too steeply but don't catch it right away? The airplane turns faster than standard rate, and when you finally spot it, because you either turned past the target heading or suddenly realize that the airplane is turning at too high a rate, you tighten up your hand on the wheel, pucker up your fanny, and jam your feet on the rudders. Almost in a panic to get the airplane back on course you turn the ailerons hard the other way, too hard. You get yourself to the point where you cannot feel the airplane anymore. Finally you notice that you went by the required heading again in the other direction. Meanwhile, your altitude usually comes unglued as well because you don't feel the change, nor do you see it in the airspeed indicator or altimeter. You are too busy staring at the directional gyro trying to get the heading right.

While all airplanes are controlled in the same manner, each type has its own interesting differences. The layout of the instrument panel normally differs somewhat from airplane to airplane, and even among airplanes of the same type but different model years. In the early days of instrument flying only one set of instruments was installed, and usually that was in the center of the panel where a pilot sitting in the left or right seat could view them. Toward the end of World War II dual instrument panels in aircraft that required more than one pilot became the norm. Manufacturers of light general aviation aircraft were slow to consider the layout of instrument panels important, and even into the late 1960s some manufacturers were still building airplanes with no apparent consideration given to the configuration of the panel.

Figure 1
Author's '57 172 instrument panel layout. It was difficult to fly IFR.

In the late 1980s I owned a 1957 Cessna 172 that I flew IFR occasionally. It still had its original instrument panel layout though the direction indicator had been updated (see Figure 1). The attitude indicator was on the right side of center where a pilot in either seat could refer to it. The direction indicator was to the left of the attitude indicator. The turn and bank was to its left and then the airspeed indicator. In the lower row, under the attitude indicator was the vertical speed indicator, then the altimeter to its left. It was a hodgepodge of instrumentation and difficult to scan.

Subsequent to that airplane being built a standard instrument layout was adopted by all aircraft manufacturers. It is what you see in most general aviation aircraft today, though many of the older types, like my 172, still have their original layouts. The new configuration is much easier for a pilot to scan (see Figure 2). The flight instruments are grouped into two rows of three instruments each. The airspeed indicator is on the left side of the panel, with the attitude indicator in the center of the top row, and the altimeter on the right side. In the bottom row are the turn coordinator or turn and bank indicator on the left side, the directional indicator in the center, and the vertical speed on the right. The six instruments are strategically placed directly in front of the pilot, and scanning this configuration is much easier than the old layouts where there was no rhyme or reason to them, except that their placement was convenient for a manufacturer who had to keep the unseen portion of the instruments clear of the flight control systems behind the panel.

Most airplanes become customized to one degree or another as they pass from owner to owner. Sometimes the instrument configuration is changed. For example, one instrument that is seen more frequently in light general aviation aircraft is the horizontal situation indicator (HSI; see Figure 3). The HSI combines navigation information and the directional indicator into one instrument. It is very useful because it reduces the number of instruments the pilot must scan, and is especially helpful during instrument approaches for that reason.

So, when you move from the cockpit of one aircraft to that of another you are liable to find a whole different atmosphere, even if the airplane is of the same type you are used to flying. What that means is, if you launch on an instrument flight without being certain of the layout your instrument scan is likely to suffer and your overall flying will do the same. If you are a student instrument pilot who flies more than one airplane during your training regime, even if they are the same make and model, you might be hampered somewhat by

Figure 2
The author's current airplane, a 1975 Piper Arrow.
It is much easier to fly IFR.

Figure 3
Horizontal Situation Indicator

the difference in instrument or equipment layouts.

*A thorough inspection of the instruments
and system layout is mandatory before a
flight in the clouds.*

Pilots don't need to add to the difficulty of instrument flight. A thorough inspection of the instruments and system layout is mandatory before a flight in
the clouds. In fact, if there are enough differences between the airplane you normally fly and the one you
are going to use on a particular trip, assuming they are
the same make and model, get a flight instructor or
another pilot who can help reduce the workload to ac-
company you, or take the airplane on a VFR flight first
so you can be certain you know the location of everything you will need.

Right after I got my multi-engine rating I went
to work for an FBO in Rhode Island selling airplanes.
After a short time they asked me to do some fill-in charter work in their Cessna 310 and pilot services for customers who owned their own airplanes.

One of the first airplanes I checked out in was a
Cessna 210 that belonged to a local company and was
used to transport their customers, employees, and occasionally family members. A flight instructor gave
me a checkride in the airplane, but he was in a hurry to
get back for a revenue student. He neglected to show
me where the landing gear hydraulic pump circuit
breaker was, or inform me that the breaker had popped
occasionally in the past, though he may not have had
that information himself.

Naturally, the first flight I did in the airplane

was in IFR conditions. I departed North Central State Airport for the Waterbury-Oxford Airport in western Connecticut with one passenger. I enjoyed the flight over immensely, because the 210, a 1972 model, was nearly new and the smoothest, most stable aircraft I had yet flown on instruments.

The ceiling at my destination was about 300 feet and the visibility 1 mile. I was looking forward to the approach, and felt I was sufficiently prepared for it. The New York Center controller vectored me to the final approach course for the ILS to Runway 36, and as the glide slope needle started its journey toward the center of the ILS indicator I selected the gear down. The whine of the electro-hydraulic motor began, the landing gear unlocked, then the motor stopped after 2 or 3 seconds of operation. It was like being hit with a baseball bat on the back side of the head. The fun flight had turned into something different. I tried recycling the gear, but knew that would not accomplish anything. I put the gear handle back in the down position because I knew the gear was unlocked, and I hoped that Mr. Murphy would take pity on me, being a low-time instrument pilot, and restore the gear to operation. He didn't.

I was too close to the runway to try to fix the problem and fly the approach, so I opted for a holding pattern while I sorted it out. I had taken a quick look at the circuit breaker panel and didn't see any breakers that were popped.

Once established in the hold I started looking further. I could not find a breaker for the landing gear hydraulic motor on the strip under the pilot's instrument panel. I knew there had to be one, so I looked everywhere. I must have looked at it four times before I saw it on the pedestal, a black circuit breaker poking through a small hole in the black panel below the throttle quadrant. I pushed it in and the motor came alive again. This time it operated through the entire gear cycle. I was greatly relieved to see the green light that indicated the gear was down and safe to land on. I returned to the ILS and completed the approach to a safe landing.

I had learned an important lesson. I had cruised through the airplane's owner's manual before the checkout and paid little attention to the picture of the panel layout. It looked like a standard Cessna panel to me. In those days the manuals were not that good. The systems descriptions left a lot to be desired, and the 210's manual described the operation of the landing gear, mentioned the circuit breaker, but didn't say where it was located. One would assume it was on the circuit breaker panel. It was not. Only the picture of the panel installation showed the breaker's location, and I didn't look close enough to see that.

If you are not scanning the instruments, the airplane is flying you. And the airplane is dumb.

So, what has that got to do with instrument scanning? Remember, the core of instrument flying is scanning the instruments. If you are not doing that the airplane is flying you. And the airplane is dumb. It doesn't know where it wants to go or how high it needs to be or how to do an instrument approach. So when you do what I did and fly an airplane you don't completely understand, you could be asking for serious trouble.

Distractions are the bane of instrument pilots, and we will discuss them further in another chapter. But remember that when you are in the clouds anything that happens, whether it is ordinary and expected or a full blown emergency and totally unexpected, will demand your attention. That means your focus will be drawn away from the instruments. If you are not quite as proficient as you should be, watch out! The old adage, "fly the airplane first," applies. So keep your eyes on the gages and prioritize the rest.

It may take you a while to realize just how important your scanning is to instrument flying, how many things it can affect, and how many things can affect it. If you already have your instrument rating and are having any of the problems I mentioned, or if your basic instrument flying is not as good as you would like, your problem probably relates to how you scan the gages. Get a good instrument flight instructor and get out there and work on it.

CHAPTER THREE

AWARENESS

When the airlines began acquiring jet air-craft, with them came the installation of cockpit voice recorders. After several accidents where investigators listened to the tapes of cockpit conversations between crew members it became apparent that a major problem concerned the lack of awareness on the part of the pilots. It did not take long to figure out that perhaps many of the general aviation accidents that occurred could be the result of the same affliction, though there was no way to know for sure because light aircraft did not have cockpit voice recorders and most of the accident airplanes were flown by one pilot.

Awareness is a broad subject that covers much of what a pilot knows and does from the time of planning a flight until it is safely concluded with the airplane secured. Involved in your awareness of a particular flight is the weather and the briefing you receive before you even set foot in the aircraft. Your physical and psychological limitations and condition, the condition of the aircraft you are to fly, knowledge of the ATC system, and the rules for operating within it are just some of details the that need to be contemplated and resolved during the flight.

The level of a pilot's awareness will affect his or her decision making capabilities, and bad decisions result in what accident investigators refer to as the "error chain." That is a chain of events that leads to an accident. Breaking the error chain by discovering even one of the faults will usually change the outcome.

For example, the first "link" in the error chain could be an improperly acknowledged clearance. Misunderstood communications can lead to other pilot actions and decisions, links in the error chain, that eventually result in an accident or incident. From the time a trip is contemplated until it is over certain operations must be prioritized and acted on as necessary.

There is a difference between awareness preceding and during a flight.

While awareness begins on the ground before the flight, there is a difference between awareness preceding and during flight. Before the flight begins most of what you do is mental. You check the weather and decide if it is suitable for you to launch on the planned flight. Considerable thought must be given to what is probably the most important decision of the day. Is it safe to fly? Are there reported or forecast icing or thunderstorms along your route of flight that will prevent you from completing the trip? Are there suitable alternates available? Will the conditions that appear to be out there allow you to complete the flight within your established personal limits?

And under the aegis of safe flight comes the condition of the aircraft. While the preflight inspection is a physical act, you need to make decisions about anything you find that could affect the flight. For example, discovering that an airplane is out of annual inspection is cause for canceling the flight until the work is done. But there may be other decisions that will not require the cancellation of the flight, but a determination of how they affect its safety.

As you go through these exercises in preparing for the flight you build a data bank in your brain of information that may be vital, or at least useful, later on. There is already an awareness at work, and if you are cautious and operate under the banner of professionalism your awareness level will be satisfactory as flight time approaches and you take the left seat.

Even as you start your engine(s) and taxi to the runway you are exercising your own brand of awareness. Is the oil pressure normal? Do the avionics exhibit their usual characteristics as they are powered up? You have a sense of what is normal and what is not, and you should look for anything out of the ordinary that might cause problems once the airplane becomes airborne. The use of a good checklist in all preflight activity will assist you in rooting out any deficiencies that may exist before the aircraft leaves the ground.

In flight there is more to keep the brain busy. Scanning the instruments and forming a mental picture of the airplane's attitude and altitude is the top priority, while manipulating the controls as required, determining the aircraft's present position, keeping abreast of changes that might occur, and making decisions that might be required are not far behind. If you let any of those factors get too far out of your grasp, situations that could result in an accident are likely to develop. Remember, an error chain begins with one event, the first link, and continues as other decisions and actions add more links to the chain.

One way to understand the concept of awareness is to think of your brain as a multi-faceted computer that has a limit to the speed at which it can process information and to the amount of data it can store. Then consider that your performance inside the cockpit - that is, how proficient you are at flying on the gages - is a major factor in determining how much information your brain can absorb.

It is not possible to decide to scan the instruments faster.

The speed at which you scan the instruments and form the mental picture necessary to determine the aircraft's relationship to the earth will determine your awareness level while airborne. And remember that it is not possible to decide to scan the instruments faster. That is a skill that is learned with the passage of time and continuous experience. An instrument pilot's first priority is scanning the instruments and keeping the aircraft upright and on the path prescribed by the clearance issued by ATC.

One who is weak at that skill will require more time and brain power to complete the ongoing task. That will leave less time and "computer memory" in reserve for other important activities or decisions. And if for any reason the pilot fixates on a single instrument, the brain sends out a busy signal, and it cannot accept any other information. It is like the computer that gets stuck in a loop.

While scanning is the chief occupation of the pilot in the clouds, that task is not the sole reason for awareness problems. Outside influences, like business or personal problems, fatigue, illness, and other physiological or psychological problems, can have a detrimental effect on one's awareness.

There is awareness and there is awareness. Take, for example, the task of flying an airplane in VFR weather conditions. As you learn to fly, your awareness level is high as you try to absorb every detail that affects your performance. As time goes on and you feel more comfortable in the aircraft you are flying, your awareness level actually decreases. It is not necessary any longer to maintain it at the previous level because you have a good grasp of what is going on around you, a better understanding of how to fly the airplane and how it will react to your control inputs, and confidence that you know what to do if something should go wrong.

The same is true of instrument flying. At the beginning of your training your awareness level will be very high as you work hard to control the airplane and manage everything else that goes along with it. While you are learning you will add tasks to your workload as your brain has the time and capacity to absorb them. So, as you gain experience you relax because you understand more of what you are doing. Your awareness level drops, while your workload remains the same. But after getting your instrument rating if you don't fly on the gages regularly, when you do your awareness level will be forced to return to the old, higher level just to keep the airplane on a straight and level path in the sky, and the brain will have to hang out the busy signal more often. When that happens you are not absorbing other things that are going on around you that can mean the difference between a safe flight and an accident.

The pilot in instrument flight literally has his or her hands and mind full.

The pilot in instrument flight literally has his or her hands and mind full. He or she is constantly scanning the flight instruments for attitude, position, and altitude. But at the same time it is necessary to consider all the other factors that impact an IFR flight. There are calls to and from ATC, weather, fuel calculations, systems checks, changes to clearances, and navigation. And that is to say nothing of any unusual problems, from a light bulb that does not operate to a passenger who suddenly becomes ill.

Here is an example. Years ago I was flying a Cessna 310 from Providence, Rhode Island to Latrobe, Pennsylvania. From shortly after takeoff until shortly before touchdown I was in the clouds. It was a very busy time for New York Center, and there was incessant chatter on the frequency between ATC and airborne aircraft. I was at 6,000 feet while a company Cessna 402, also bound for Latrobe, was just ahead of me at 8,000 feet.

As I approached an intersection along Victor 93 I noticed that the minimum enroute altitude (MEA) changed from 6,000 to 8,000 feet. I did not know precisely how far ahead the other aircraft was, so I was not sure if the controller would let me climb or if I would have to hold until there was enough separation. As I closed on the intersection I became concerned that the controller had not addressed the situation. When there was a break in the chatter I queried the controller about the MEA change and received this crisp reply: "95 Quebec, climb immediately to 8,000 feet."

The controller had failed to notice that an altitude change was in order until I called his attention to it.

The word immediately, when used by a controller, means do it yesterday, so I climbed quickly to my new altitude without wondering how far ahead the other aircraft was. Obviously it was far enough. The controller, being as busy as he was, had failed to notice that an altitude change was in order until I called his attention to it. If I had not been keeping abreast of the potential for change along the route of flight it is possible that safety could have been jeopardized.

One reason that awareness is important is because pilots and controllers are supposed to check each other. If one makes a mistake the other should catch it. If a pilot's brain space is so tied up with flying his or her airplane that he or she does not pay any attention to whatever else is going on those checks and balances are lost.

That kind of awareness is vital during vectors for an instrument approach. The pilot should have enough time and brain space available to know where he or she is in relation to the airport at all times. Why is that necessary? What if the radar goes out of service while the controller is vectoring you? The controller will probably come back with holding instructions, and you will have to carry them out. But you cannot do that if you don't know your position.

Or, what if the controller has just come on duty and misjudges the wind while vectoring you to final approach? If you go through the localizer and are too close to the final fix to get the airplane lined up you will need to abandon the approach. But if you don't have any idea how far from the fix you are, you could wind up in a dangerous predicament or feel forced to intercept the glide slope when you have not yet got the localizer under control or the airplane configured properly. Your workload will increase, and that will take more time and brain space.

Partial panel means you will need to get the same amount of information with fewer instruments.

System failures will increase your workload, especially if they involve the flight instruments. Even a potential failure should be enough to raise your awareness level to a higher state as you continue to monitor the instrument or indicator that relates the condition of that system. Partial panel is no fun at all and most of us are not prepared for it. You will need to get the same amount of information with fewer instruments available. Again, that means your brain space will be put to use and leave less for other tasks.

Physiological influences, such as fatigue, can have a detrimental effect on a pilot's awareness. Say you are scheduled to fly a trip that requires ten hours for the day including flying and waiting time. But the weather is bad and there are delays going and coming. Then your passengers are late. By the time you are in position to fly the ILS on the last leg of the flight you have been working for nearly 14 hours. That is a long day and the associated fatigue can be a factor in how you perceive what is going on around you.

Those in business who fly their own airplanes, in addition to having delays because of weather and other factors beyond their control, often bring outside problems into the cockpit with them, perhaps business or technical issues following a meeting. And others are not immune either. We all have problems occasionally and we must determine, before we get into the cockpit, whether they are such that they will interfere with the safe conduct of the flight.

You probably remember your basic flight instructor imploring you to "stay ahead of the aircraft" at all times. That is vital for any pilot and is associated with awareness level. Part of your brain space is used for considering all aspects of a flight and the potential for conflict or change. If that space is "borrowed" to make up for a fault somewhere else, say a slow level of scanning, then you cannot think ahead of the airplane. You are too busy just maintaining the status quo.

A good example is a change in routing issued by ATC while you are in flight. Would you just accept it without first looking at your chart and determining whether it was acceptable, would change the status of your fuel supply at the destination, or would affect any other areas that could influence the safety of flight? Such considerations are examples of thinking ahead of your airplane, and you must have the time and brain space available to handle it, or anything else that is thrown your way.

Those with the toughest job are pilots who fly by themselves and don't enjoy the benefit of an autopilot. Multi-pilot crews have a somewhat easier time of it, if they work together as a crew. But if the crew philosophy breaks down in a multi-pilot cockpit, there is great danger for the aircraft and its passengers.

There are two good examples of that phenomenon. First, years ago a DC-9, a commercial airliner, was approaching Charlotte, North Carolina. The airport was IFR and the pilots were set up for a VOR approach to Runway 36. The airplane crashed 3.3 miles short of the runway. When investigators listened to the cockpit voice recorder there was little doubt about why the accident happened.

Conducting the approach, the pilots were talking about everything except what they were doing.

The pilots, while conducting the approach, were

talking about everything except what they were doing. They chatted about the stock market, politics, their automobiles, and finally tried to locate a tower on the ground but in close proximity to the final approach course. The airplane, being flown by the first officer, crossed the final approach fix nearly 500 feet lower than it should have, then kept descending until it hit the ground. The pilots even ignored a terrain warning alert that the aircraft was only 1,000 feet above the surface.

There was no awareness in that cockpit. The airline required the pilot not flying, the Captain, to make certain callouts during the descent that included the airspeed, rate of descent, and altitude. He never did. He allowed his brain space to be cluttered by items that had no value whatsoever to the flight. Perhaps he felt that because the first officer was doing the flying he could relax and enjoy the ride. But that is not the way it works.

Another example is the more recent crash of a Jetstream 4101 in Columbus, Ohio. The Captain kept the airspeed high during his ILS approach, and when he finally decided to slow the airplane down he pulled the power levers to idle.

You would not do that in a piston-engine airplane because of the cooling effects on your engine(s), but in a turbine-engine airplane it is permissible. The autopilot was flying the airplane, and after the power reduction the crew became immersed in the landing checklist. The autopilot, set to maintain a pitch attitude, slowed the airplane, and as the gear and flaps were extended neither pilot realized that power was needed to make the airport. The airplane crashed 1.2

miles east of the airport after it stalled. There were several fatalities that included the crew.

The National Transportation Safety Board (NTSB) determined that even when the airplane stalled the accident was avoidable, but the pilots still did not react. It appears that the Captain incorrectly assumed that the tail had stalled due to icing and did not advance the power levers to maximum. Instead he raised the flaps, which only aggravated the stalled condition.

The flight crew allowed themselves to lose awareness of what the airplane was doing while they completed the landing checklist. Perhaps they had faith in the autopilot, but autopilots only do the human's bidding (see Chapter Five).

You have a lot to think about before your next instrument flight. In fact, you should sample your level of awareness at different points during that flight. This is easily done by taking a moment, looking around the airplane, thinking about what is going on and what you think is going to happen. If you can do that intentionally several times during the flight, your awareness is at a reasonable level. But if you don't have the time or brain space for that, you have a fundamental problem to correct before something happens that requires more of your attention than you have to give.

CHAPTER FOUR

POSITIONAL AWARENESS

Most pilots, at one time or another, become confused as to their position in the air-space. I am not talking about being lost, but simply disoriented for a short time. Navigating while in the clouds is not as easy as in VFR conditions because most of the time you have little or no ground reference and cannot look out the window to establish where you are.

   With more and more direct clearances being offered these days it is entirely possible that a pilot may not know his or her exact position. He or she may have a general idea where the aircraft is, but if someone were to ask for a position report, a quick cross check of the VORs or a VOR and DME would be necessary.

While the VOR is still the basis for our airways system, that will probably change in the not too distant future. The global positioning system (GPS) is rapidly becoming the accepted method of navigation, and there is even talk of shutting down the long-range navigation (Loran) system that has been the bridge between the VOR and GPS. And while GPS has great navigation value to the pilot, it makes it easier to neglect the aircraft's actual position, as opposed to the bearing and distance to the destination.

Loran and GPS are a navigational miracle. In one box a pilot can see the distance to the destination or selected fix, ground speed, bearing and track to the fix, estimated time enroute, and a host of other information that would otherwise take a great deal of calculating or searching. The great majority of the units installed in light general aviation aircraft are only certified for VFR use, but GPS boxes certified for IFR enroute and approach navigation are quickly being added to the fleet.

The information provided by the GPS or Loran is easy to use. Enter the destination airport and almost instantly you know exactly how far you are from it and what heading to fly to get there. Eventually GPS will force almost every other method of navigation we have in our airplanes into retirement. But until that happens we still have to learn to use the ILS, VOR, ADF, DME, and other traditional navigational devices.

Is it that important to know exactly where you are at a given time during IFR flight? You can bet your life on it. What if you had an engine failure, or lost communications with your ATC controller? You want someone to know where you are in the event of the former, and to reestablish contact with ATC you will have to call Flight Service or another center controller and give that person a position report.

But too many of us fly along while giving little thought to what might happen. We are content that everything is operating properly, we are flying direct to our destination and looking forward to ending the flight with an instrument approach that we are prepared to execute. When something happens that requires a quick response it often takes us a while to get geared up. When time is of the essence that extra time could be very critical to the success of the flight.

One major navigation problem is that many pilots don't understand how the VOR works.

One major navigation problem is that many pilots don't understand how a VOR works. Sure, they can navigate directly to or from a station, or along an airway, but intercepting stated radials can be a problem. Ask them what radial of a particular VOR they are presently crossing, and chances are they will give you the reciprocal to the one they are on, if they even come that close.

That is because they center the OBS needle with a "To" indication and read the azimuth, neglecting the fact that they are actually on the reciprocal of what is presented. For example, a controller in a non-radar environment asks you what radial of the XYZ VOR you are crossing. You tune in the station, center the OBS with a "To" indication, and give him the direct reading, 302 degrees. "I'm crossing the 302-degree radial," you reply. If the controller has been following your flight properly, he or she will immediately ask for a clarification, because you are really crossing the 122-degree radial southeast of the station. And if the controller takes your response at face value, he or she could clear another airplane into your airspace. That would be a very dangerous situation.

Perhaps a quick VOR refresher is called for here. If you center the needle with a "To" indication of 270 degrees that means you will fly west to get to the station or that you are east of it (see Figure 1).

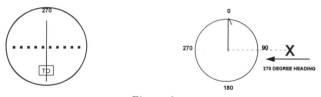

Figure 1
VOR Position Using a "To" Indication

Since radials "radiate" from the station, you are really on the 90-degree radial but flying a 270-degree heading toward it. If you use a "To" indication to establish current position on the VOR you should take the reciprocal of the indication as your current radial. Some pilots prefer, when establishing position, to center the OBS needle with a "From" indication (see Figure 2). That way you don't have to do the math, but if you plan to navigate to the station make sure you change to a "To" indication before using it. That is a very basic piloting skill, but it is amazing how many pilots don't understand how it works. Give that some thought

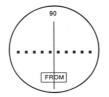

Figure 2
Same Position Using "From" Indication

before your next flight in case you are asked for a VOR position report.

Another problem instrument pilots have is keeping track of their position relative to an airport they are being vectored to for an approach. We touched on this subject in the last chapter on awareness, but we will delve a little further into it now.

Despite your perceived experience, ATC controllers want to get your flight on the ground as soon as possible. They want you out of the way because they know they have more airplanes coming. With more airplanes in their traffic sector not only do they have to work harder, but there is more chance of separation violations and collisions. If a controller vectors you a long way out on downwind it is not because he or she doesn't want you to get on the ground. It is because there is other traffic that could be a hazard to you, or that you could be a hazard to another aircraft in the sector.

I was flying a Turbo-Commander into Miami a few years ago at the end of a non-stop IFR flight from Detroit. The weather in Miami was good and I had about 45 minutes of fuel remaining when I was turned over to Miami Approach about 25 miles or so northeast of the airport. Before long I had the airport in sight and called it out to the controller. He told me to fly a 270-degree heading that put me on downwind, and to stand by. He was busy with other traffic. I flew a 20-mile downwind before being turned back to the airport for a landing to the east.

I knew where I was because I saw the airport as I went by it. But had I been in the clouds I would have had to use my nav radios to keep my position updated. Why is it so important to know your position within terminal airspace when you are being vectored for an approach? First, you cannot control your airspeed properly unless you know your precise distance from the airport, what approach is in use, and approximately how far you are from touchdown. The distance to the airport converted to time, and time to touchdown, can be two completely different things, as they were on my approach to Miami that day.

If you don't know where you are
you cannot configure the airplane
or control speed properly during
the approach.

Airspeed, if you are flying a light single, probably is not going to mean a heck of a lot. A Cessna 172 or Piper Warrior slows down quickly when the power is reduced, but airplanes like the Beech Baron or the various Mooney models don't slow down rapidly. The same is true for most turbine powered airplanes. The pilot has to think way ahead of his machine in the terminal airspace so as not to wind up flying the final at cruise airspeed. If you don't know where you are in the airspace you cannot possibly configure the airplane properly and keep the speed under control or changing as circumstances warrant during the various phases of the approach.

Planning for that approach begins long before you get to the terminal airspace. At some point before being handed off to the approach controller you will check the automatic terminal information system (ATIS) and determine what approach is in use. Then you start making plans for how you expect the vectoring and approach to work. That includes briefing yourself on the approach, knowing where you are and from what direction you are approaching, determining where you need to start slowing the airplane, and then being on the alert in case things don't go quite the way you plan them.

In high performance piston singles and twins you need to be careful while reducing power, especially in winter when it is easier to shock cool your cylinders. The same applies to light singles, but since the speed reduction is smaller, it is easier to use small power reductions to get the desired results. In the faster, more powerful piston engine airplanes, if you come blasting into the terminal airspace at cruise or nearly so, because you didn't realize you were that close to it, you will have to reduce power in large increments to get the airplane slowed down, and that could cause engine problems.

What if something happens along the route or in the terminal airspace that requires an unscheduled landing? How can you make a reasonable decision about landing short of your destination or continuing, if you don't know where you are, what airports are around you, and how long it will take to get to the original destination? It is much easier for a pilot to be aware of his or her position before something out of the ordinary happens than to suddenly be forced to come up with an accurate location in an emergency, which requires his or her attention elsewhere.

How you maintain your position depends on the radio aids along the route of flight, and the equipment aboard the aircraft. In my Piper Arrow I usually use everything I have to keep track of my enroute position. I will set the ADF to a nearby beacon and keep track of the bearing to the station until I tune to the next one. I will use the number two VOR and DME to cross check my position with that of the number one and the ADF. And though my Loran is only VFR, I will use it to maintain a distance and bearing to my destination. That way I will have, for planning, constant information on ground speed, time to the station, and when I can expect to arrive there, and still maintain a good awareness of where I am at any moment.

I use everything that is installed to keep in touch with my position.

In other airplanes that have the ability to fly direct to the destination I will use the IFR certified Loran, GPS, or area navigation (RNAV) for navigating in a straight line, while backing that up with the VORs, ADF, DME, or whatever other equipment is in the panel. Again, I normally use everything that is installed to keep in touch with my position.

Once the approach controller starts vectoring you to the final, your true position becomes more important. Like the old saying about landings, "a good landing is the result of a good approach," it extends into the realm of instrument flying. If your speed is high, you don't catch the glide slope, or you let the localizer wander, chances are your landing - should you be lucky enough to find the runway - will be just as poor as the trip from the outer marker. So knowing your exact relationship to the location of the airport is the only way you can plan for a satisfactory approach.

Good positional awareness is required when you are working with a control tower that doesn't have a radar repeater scope. The controller may ask you several times during your approach for a position report so he or she can plan to space your arrival with other approaching aircraft. Some may be VFR, if the weather is appropriate, and others IFR. You should be aware that if you break out of the clouds close to the airport there could be VFR airplanes in the pattern. The only thing the controller has to go on is your position reporting to separate your flight from others in the traffic pattern, so be certain you make the reports he or she asks for and that they are correct.

Flying instrument approaches at uncontrolled airports requires more pilot diligence because there is no one to sort out the traffic. Each pilot has to make himself or herself aware of the local traffic by monitoring the unicom or the common traffic advisory frequency (CTAF). But radios are not required and there could be someone tooling around the traffic pattern just below the clouds and you will not have any idea that he or she is there. For those that are monitoring the frequency it is very important that you give correct position reports while you are on the approach. They will fly the traffic pattern based on those reports and if one is incorrect it could lead to a midair collision.

Losing one navigation aid should not be a big problem.

Navigation radio failures contribute to pilot disorientation. If you have more than one VOR, or any other type of nav radio aboard, losing one should not be a big problem unless you are planning on a VOR or ILS approach at your destination and that is the one that decides to go to sleep. Today, most instrument equipped airplanes have two VORs, an ADF, a DME, and Loran or GPS. So there is no reason why a pilot should not be capable of maintaining positional awareness with the loss of one piece of equipment. Some Lorans and GPS receivers have battery backups, so even if you lose your entire electrical system you can still navigate. I carry a hand-held GPS with me for that reason.

While you are enroute, controllers may vector you around traffic or weather that you don't want to get into. Any time you get off the intended route for any length of time it is important that you keep track of your position. I have, over the years, been forgotten by controllers after receiving a "vector around traffic." That can lead to airspace and separation violations. While they are not your fault, if you collide with an Air Force F-16 because a controller forgot about you and vectored you into a restricted area, you are just as dead as if you made the mistake yourself. So keep track of where you are, even when you are being vectored, and query a controller if you suspect he or she has forgotten you or if you are approaching any kind of special-use airspace.

If you have a Loran or GPS aboard it is easy to keep track of your position during extended vectors. Just set the receiver on an airport or fix that is near your present position. You will always have a bearing and distance from it, and a glance at the instrument chart will locate your position. If the vectoring continues for any length of time you can tune the radio to another fix in your vicinity. GPS or Lorans that have moving map displays keep you visually updated and make it easy for you to keep track of your position.

Positional awareness helps you keep clear of rising terrain.

One major reason for following your position as the flight progresses is to keep clear of rising terrain. Controlled flight into terrain has always been a problem for instrument aircraft, and those piloted by professionals and non-professionals alike have been a victim of this phenomenon. One major accident happened when the crew of a DC-8 decided to hold over Salt Lake City while trying to solve an electrical fault that had taken much of the airplane's electrical equipment off line. The crew allowed the airplane to drift into an area of high terrain, outside its assigned holding pattern, where it crashed. Controllers were trying to reach the crew to warn them, but the pilots were off the frequency talking to their maintenance base on their only available radio when the accident took place.

This accident should remind you about situational awareness as well as proper navigation. The DC-8 crew's awareness was not satisfactory. In effect, no one was flying the airplane because none of the crew members were aware of its position. And when contact with controllers was broken to discuss the problem with company maintenance personnel the crew was totally responsible for knowing where the airplane was and that it was clear of the high terrain. But none of the pilots did the job. Perhaps they were overly reliant on radar to keep them out of trouble, or they just got so involved in their problem that none of the pilots realized that no one was flying the airplane.

When you are flying VFR you can allow some slight distractions to occur, such as talking to the pilot or passenger seated next to you. But when you are in the clouds anything that takes your attention away from the job at hand can severely impact the safety of flight. One of the many responsibilities the instrument pilot has is navigating to the destination. It is vital to know the aircraft's position throughout the flight whether it is under radar supervision or not. You have only one airplane to worry about while an ATC controller has many. Don't rely on him or her to keep you out of trouble.

CHAPTER FIVE

USING THE AUTOPILOT

Most of us enjoy flying our airplanes on instruments. But there are times when the workload is heavy and we need a hand. An operating autopilot can be our savior. But an autopilot will perform only as it is directed. That means it can be a lifesaver or a killer depending on how you program it and monitor its progress.

There are all kinds of autopilots out there from wing levelers to full-blown units that do everything but chew your gum for you. You will probably have little choice in what you get because autopilots are expensive and most people usually maintain whatever comes in the airplane they buy.

That is the case with my Piper Arrow. It has a factory installed Piper Autocontrol IIIB, which is simply a wing leveler with a heading-hold function. It also couples to the VORs and localizer. It does not have a pitch control or altitude hold. I would not upgrade it because I enjoy flying the airplane manually and use the autopilot only when my attention must be diverted from the instruments for a short period.

What if the autopilot quits working?

But too many pilots rely too much on their autopilots when they are in the clouds. Those who are not proficient enough may take off thinking the autopilot will keep them out of trouble, and that probably occurs more often than we like to think. But what if the autopilot quits working for one reason or another?

We have discussed at some length in earlier chapters how important scanning the instruments is and how slow scanning influences awareness. A pilot who is slow to scan because he or she is rusty, or flying a new type of airplane and not yet comfortable with its operation, should not rely on the autopilot to keep things on the straight and level. But I have flown with many pilots who simply turn the autopilot on right after takeoff and shut it off just before touchdown, hardly ever touching the controls. In addition to taking a chance on the autopilot failing, pilots who let "George" do most of the work for them will never maintain whatever instrument proficiency they do have, though it is perfectly legal to log that time as instrument time toward legal currency.

The operation of most autopilots is similar in that the pilot pushes a few buttons to activate the modes he or she wants to use. Late model autopilots that include a pitch control usually power up in whatever attitude the airplane happens to be flying. For example, if you are climbing when you engage the autopilot and heading hold it will maintain the designated heading and climb at the current pitch attitude, which means the airspeed will decrease as the aircraft continues its climb. Then, when you get to your cruise altitude you engage the altitude hold mode, if it is so equipped. The autopilot should maintain the cruise altitude.

Earlier autopilots were a little different. I fly an older Navajo that still has its original Piper Altimatic III autopilot. To engage it in a climb or descent you must manually turn the pitch trim wheel until the trim indicator signifies that the autopilot is aligned with the pitch attitude of the aircraft. Engaging the pitch control before making that adjustment will result in the airplane pitching up or down depending on where the pitch trim wheel is set. That can generate much discomfort among the passengers. The same is true for level flight when engaging the altitude hold mode.

Autopilots that don't have a pitch or altitude hold mode, like the one in my Arrow, are pretty simple to operate. There are two switches and a roll control knob on the face of the unit (see Figure 1). The left switch is the wing leveler or power-on switch. When that is engaged the unit will keep the wings level. The switch on the right is the heading hold mode. When that is selected the airplane will turn to the heading at which the "bug" on the directional gyro is set. The roll control feature overrides both functions and will turn the airplane at a bank angle up to standard rate depending on how far you turn the knob. Some autopilots will turn in a steeper bank in one direction than the other when using the roll control, but the angle of bank is subject to adjustment, and a good radio shop can easily tweak the unit so it works satisfactorily.

Figure 1
Piper Autocontrol IIIB

When using any autopilot, whether it has altitude hold or not, the pilot must be very careful to maintain the altitude that was assigned by ATC. Center and approach control facilities now have "snitch alarms" that alert controllers when an airplane is more than 300 feet from its assigned altitude. When the alarm goes off the controller will ask the pilot to confirm the altimeter reading he or she is seeing. If the pilot tells the controller the wrong thing it is an automatic violation.

It is very easy for an autopilot that is not properly monitored to get you in trouble with the snitch alarm. For example, if you are cruising along and disconnect the altitude hold to correct for a new altimeter setting, change the pitch attitude slightly and then forget it, it will not take long for the airplane to deviate 300 feet, though it depends on the rate of climb or descent you have selected. I have seen pilots forget to level out at the assigned cruise altitude during climb or descent because they were doing something else instead of monitoring the instruments as vigilantly as they should.

Autopilots without an altitude hold or pitch control mode can get you into trouble also, because they require constant monitoring to maintain altitude. You will need to change the aircraft's pitch trim as required, and if the airplane starts to climb or descend and you don't make a correction it will not take long to gain or lose 300 feet. Turbulence or gusts can keep you on your toes. It is very easy to overcorrect with the trim wheel and go right through your assigned altitude when making corrections. Even in light turbulence I find that it is easier to hand fly an airplane that is not equipped with altitude hold. Whether you agree with that will probably depend on whether you are a mechanical instrument pilot or one who uses feedback from the aircraft to assist in controlling it.

It is easy to overcontrol altitude
via manual trim with the autopilot
operating.

The problem with using manual pitch trim while the autopilot is operating is that unless you hold onto the control wheel there is little pitch feedback, the kind that you normally use to maintain altitude in manual flight. Electric trim, if your airplane is so equipped, is very slow to respond to your inputs. If you try to control altitude via the manual trim it is very easy to overcontrol, resulting in up-and-down oscillations.

Many autopilots will maintain a VOR radial or fly a localizer during an approach. But that feature in the lower cost autopilots often does not work that well. It is so sensitive that the slightest movement of the VOR needle forces the autopilot to make a correction. That means that the airplane is constantly rolling back and forth, which becomes more uncomfortable the closer you get to the station. I prefer to use the heading hold and make corrections as they are needed.

The signals coming out of GPS units are more stable than those from VORs. Autopilots coupled to them fly a better course line with much less needle chasing. Like RNAV the course width of the signal is wider than that of a VOR so the needle is less sensitive.

Most autopilots are programmed
to shut themselves off when
certain gust loads are encountered.

Most autopilots are programmed to shut themselves off when certain gust loads are encountered, to prevent them from overloading the airframe by making a correction too quickly. That is precisely what happened over the Pacific in 1992 when a China Airlines MD-11-P encountered moderate turbulence that initially affected control of the aircraft around its roll axis. The autopilot shut itself down and apparently the aircraft's captain overcontrolled the airplane and it stalled at least four times before a complete recovery was made. There is more to the story, which involves that type of aircraft's center of gravity position at high altitude cruise, and the fact that the pilots were relatively new to the aircraft. But in most cases when the autopilot shuts down an experienced pilot will make nominal corrections against the gusting forces.

The autopilot was inadvertently
shut off by one of the crew members.

Accidents have been caused by pilots who relied on their autopilot system to fly their airplane but failed to monitor it closely. A classic accident occurred in the Everglades of Florida in the early 1970s. The Lockheed L-1011 crew was setting up for an approach to Miami. When the pilots extended the landing gear the nose wheel safe light did not illuminate. The airplane was being flown by its autopilot at 2,000 feet. While the entire crew attempted to locate the problem the aircraft descended into the ground. Investigators determined that the autopilot was inadvertently shut off by one of the crewmembers, and the airplane descended at a rate of 500 feet per minute into the Everglades. That means that for four minutes no one looked at the aircraft's instruments, nor was anyone flying the airplane. It turned out that the problem with the faulty gear indication was a burned-out light bulb.

Another accident occurred more recently. It involved a Piper Aztec with three persons on board, who spent a day flying from Palm Beach, Florida to Groton, Connecticut. The pilot received a complete weather briefing from Miami Flight Service before departure. The destination was forecast to be low IFR for the entire day. The pilot phoned the FBO at Groton, where he was based, and asked what the weather was like. Someone told him it was 300 and 1. He arranged for transportation for himself and his passengers at Providence, Rhode Island, because he expected to land there instead of Groton. Apparently Groton's ILS approach was out of service that day.

On arrival in the Groton area the pilot was informed that the ceiling was obscured at 100 feet and the visibility 1/4 mile. He elected to try the VOR approach to Runway 23 and declared his intention to go to Providence when he missed it.

ATC vectored the Aztec to the final and cleared it for the approach. The pilot was advised that a Cherokee had tried the approach twice and failed to get in. After passing the final approach fix, Babet Intersection, the pilot descended to his minimum descent altitude and engaged his autopilot. Then he focused his attention out the window while he and his passenger-pilot searched for the airport. Neither of them looked at the instruments again. The aircraft kept descending until it collided with some trees and then the ground. The pilot and one passenger received minor injuries in the accident while the other passenger was injured seriously.

The pilot told investigators that he expected the altitude hold feature of his autopilot to maintain the selected altitude, but it did not. Why? It could be that after flying all day he was fatigued and anxious to get on the ground. In his quest to look out the window and locate the airport he may have forgotten to engage the altitude hold mode.

If you rely on an autopilot, especially during an approach or any time you are close to the ground, you need to keep an eye on what it is doing. Don't be lulled into complacency because your electronic co-pilot is flying the airplane. It will only do what you tell it, and if you tell it the wrong thing an unplanned descent, similar to the misfortune of these two aircraft, or some other equally upsetting and hazardous situation could result. Remember, neither accident was caused by the autopilot but by the inattention of the pilots to their operation.

You must be thoroughly familiar with the intricacies of your autopilot and its functions. Some autopilots will maintain a particular pitch attitude while others will maintain an airspeed in a climb or descent. A few will do either. If you are climbing at a given pitch attitude the indicated airspeed will drop as the climb continues and the power in a non-turbocharged aircraft drops. If you don't change the pitch attitude to maintain airspeed, the airplane will eventually stall. In a turbo-charged airplane the same will occur only at a higher altitude. In a descent the airspeed will increase, and if not checked it can reach destructive speeds.

An autopilot that maintains airspeed will vary the pitch of the aircraft to maintain whatever speed you have selected. In a climb the autopilot may do a series of oscillations if not monitored. For example, you select a speed of 120 knots in the climb. To maintain that speed the autopilot has to reduce pitch as the altitude increases. When the pitch attitude gets close to level flight the airspeed will try to increase, and the autopilot will respond by increasing pitch, then decreasing it again as the speed drops. In a descent it will do the same, adjusting the pitch so the airspeed remains stable. If you are looking for a 140-knot speed in the descent, as your altitude decreases the airspeed will try to increase, commanding a pitch-up from the auto-pilot. Again, the aircraft could level out and attempt to do a series of oscillations under certain conditions.

Many functions an instrument pilot must perform would be difficult without an autopilot to assist. Routing changes are one. Trying to locate an airway or fix that is not on the section of the chart immediately in front of you will require much of your attention for a short period. And that can get you into trouble if you engage the autopilot haphazardly.

I was flying a Cessna 402 from Hilton Head, South Carolina to Providence, Rhode Island one night in IFR conditions when I was issued an amendment to my clearance. I took out the chart and started looking for my new routing after engaging the autopilot. The Washington Center controller was very busy and it was not long before he called and asked if I was turning west. I didn't look at the instruments before replying that I was on course. I was too busy trying to find an airway that I was not familiar with. In fact, I was a little upset at being given that routing. I was very familiar with most of the IFR routes up and down the coast, but that was one I had never been issued.

The direction indicator had failed and the autopilot was following it around in circles.

It was not long before the controller called back and told me I was turning south. This time I put the chart down and looked at the direction indicator (DI). I was flying in circles. The DI had failed and the autopilot was following it around in circles. Since that day I have never covered up the instruments by opening a chart so that it blocks the panel, nor will I allow anyone sitting in the right seat to do that in an airplane I am flying.

An autopilot is useful when copying a revised clearance or checking enroute weather, and during discussions with passengers about enroute planning for weather or other factors that could impact their plans. When something out of the ordinary occurs that requires more of a pilot's attention, it can be a big help. A fault in the retractable landing gear system, for example, requires troubleshooting. If recycling the gear does not solve it, the autopilot will allow you to direct more attention toward the problem, but don't forget to monitor it carefully, something the L-1011 pilots in Florida failed to do. Remember, when you don't monitor the autopilot and the airplane's progress, the airplane is flying you, you are not flying it.

I think of the autopilot as an aid. It is a tool that I have to manage during flight that can make instrument flying easier and safer if used properly. Some pilots are enamored of the autopilot and its abilities. They use it for the majority of their flying and hardly ever touch the controls themselves. Approach couplers will fly a localizer and glide slope but only if the other instruments are monitored continuously. If the airspeed drops, as it did just before the Jetstream accident at Columbus when the pilot pulled the throttles back to idle, the airplane will attempt to stay on course and eventually stall. If there is turbulence on final approach the autopilot may shut off if the gust loading is too high. Will you know it if it does?

Most autopilots have some kind of audio or visual alert that tells you when the autopilot has shut itself down. It should be checked before flight for functionality, but don't rely on it. Monitor the instruments whenever you use the autopilot.

In the 26 years I have been flying I have used an approach coupler no more than a few times and those were only to check the operation of the device in a particular airplane. I cannot maintain my proficiency and currency if I don't fly approaches myself, though I can log autopilot-flown approaches. And those pilots who fly IFR only sporadically must guard against relying on an approach coupler instead of their own ability to fly the aircraft on any approach that is required.

Today, a pilot is a systems manager, but just how far do you want to carry that description? Flying on the gages is not an easy task for most of us, and we work hard at keeping up with everything that occurs during an instrument flight. But where do you draw the line between relying on your autopilot or yourself in the clouds? Each of us will answer the question differently, and I suspect that confidence, currency, and proficiency will drive that determination.

CHAPTER SIX

PROFESSIONALISM

Pilots get their instrument ratings so they can get more use out of their airplanes as well as further their aviation careers. There are too many days when the weather prevents a VFR pilot from flying, especially when he or she needs to make a long cross-country trip for business or some other purpose that requires being at a particular location at a given time.

Just because you have the ability to fly in IFR conditions does not mean that you can go in any kind of weather. I am reminded of the businessman who bought an Aztec years ago and hired a pilot to fly it for him. The salesman told him the airplane was suitable for all-weather flying so the new owner wanted to go in all weather. He did not keep pilots very long because of his demanding schedule and his inability to accept the fact that he could not fly on a given day because of weather.

The airplane flew into the terrain, and both the pilot and the businessman were killed.

One time he pushed his pilot to get in the air as quickly as possible and the pilot used the wrong runway at an uncontrolled airport. Just as the airplane lifted off another Aztec was doing the same on the advertised runway and the two pilots barely avoided a collision at the intersection. But the predictable end to that businessman's saga arrived one day when he pushed his new, young, inexperienced pilot to bust minimums during a VOR approach into the home airport. The airplane flew into the terrain, and both the pilot and the businessman were killed.

None of us sets out to cause an accident and kill ourselves or our passengers, but many of the accidents we read about are caused by circumstances that can be avoided. For example, at what point is building time toward a better job more important than taking every precaution possible to fly safely? The constant badgering of the boss to get him where he wants to go on time has to be put on the back burner if the weather is not suitable. If you get fired because he's unhappy, think of the guy who pushed his pilots until one of them flew him into the ground. It is not worth your life, or his for that matter, to be flying when you know you should not be.

I know professional pilots whose professionalism is lacking, and private pilots who act like real professionals.

Your level of professionalism determines how you conduct yourself when making the decisions necessary for any flight. There are many professional pilots out there who fly day after day in all kinds of weather. Over the years I have run across some of them whose professionalism was sorely lacking. At the same time, I know private pilots who act like real professionals, though they may be flying a Cessna 172 or some other light airplane instead of the heavier corporate "iron."

The kind of airplane you fly matters not. What is important is how you conduct yourself in and out of the cockpit with respect to making the judgment calls and other decisions that are necessary for safe flight. Sometimes it means standing up to a bullying boss - yes, at the risk of losing your job. It means having standards that are not arbitrarily changed to suit the conditions you encounter.

Standards make the difference between a pilot with professionalism and one without. One pilot's standards may allow a takeoff during a raging snowstorm into icing conditions with an airplane that lacks any ice protection equipment. The other's would leave him or her sitting home reading a book by a fire, waiting for the weather to move on.

The pilot who stays home probably has lofty standards in everything he or she does. Everything is accomplished with pride in seeing it done right. And from those standards comes a set of personal limits that reflect the pilot's abilities, confidence level, and experience.

The pilot who departs in the raging snowstorm is bound more by an urge to get to the destination, and considers that proof of his or her worth.

The pilot who does not fly in the snowstorm is more likely to be fanatical about checking the weather, planning the route to the nth degree, and making certain that the airplane is up to the task. The other pilot probably will give little thought to the weather. After all, if there is a raging snowstorm at the takeoff point the weather has to get better anywhere else, doesn't it? He or she probably files direct to the destination whether the airplane has some form of long range navigation or not and figures ATC will sort out the routing. That means that there is little planning done in advance of a flight. That pilot is so good that there is no need to worry about the condition of the airplane. If anything goes wrong he or she is up to the task and will bring the airplane, crew, and passengers back safely. Too often, though, it does not work that way.

Certificates and ratings have nothing to do with professionalism.

Understand that pilot certificates and ratings have nothing to do with professionalism. It is one's determination, attitude toward flying, and probably life in general, that brings forth the commodity. A pilot with a high standard of professionalism will not allow decision making to be influenced by passengers or others with an interest in seeing a flight depart on time. And sometimes it is difficult.

A charter or freight pilot has the responsibility for deciding whether to begin a flight or not. On one side the boss is tugging at him or her because the revenue from the trip will help the company's bottom line. The passengers are eager to be underway because they are paying for the trip and want to get to their destination on time. In the back of the pilot's mind is the FAA and the myriad of regulations that he or she is responsible for adhereing to. But the FAA is not there breathing down the pilot's neck, while the passengers and boss are.

Are one person's standards or personal limits suitable for everyone? Probably not. Some may consider their standards adequate because of years of experience, while others are less confident and require more thoroughness to reduce the possibility of problems arising while airborne. Which pilot is right? They both are. Each person sets his or her own standards and personal limits, though the input of others may be invaluable in helping a pilot develop a professional attitude. You may find observing someone else plan and fly a trip or series of trips, or even local hangar flying sessions, to be very helpful.

Your professionalism is put to the test constantly. For instance, you are flying a cross-country IFR trip from your home base to Grandma's birthday party. You have five hours of fuel on board for a 4-hour flight. The winds aloft are stronger than forecast and you are looking at an extra half hour enroute. But that will leave you with only 30 minutes of fuel when you get to your destination.

You know the weather is stable. It has been running around 600 feet and 2 miles since you started checking it earlier in the day. The forecast has a chance of 300 and 1 included in it, but that has not material-ized. Do you take a chance that you will not need more than 30 minutes of extra fuel and keep going, or do you stop and fill the tanks?

Pilots whose engine(s) quit close to their final destination usually arrive at that predicament because they keep putting off the decision to stop for fuel until they finally decide they can make it, albeit with little left for anything but a straight-in approach. Anything out of the ordinary that occurs, like being number 7 in line for the approach after a runway change that re-quires vectors to the other side of the airport, will com-plicate matters greatly as well as increase the pilot's anxiety. Sometimes the pilot will confess to ATC and, it is hoped, get on the ground before the fuel runs out, but too often he or she is as silent as the engine(s) be-comes.

Would you let that happen on your flight to Grandma's? The pilot with a professional attitude will accept the fuel stop, though it will cost some time and inconvenience for the rest of the family, both those aboard the airplane and those waiting at the destination airport. He or she will have a personal limit that will not allow the flight to continue with less than a prede-termined amount of fuel on board. After the fuel stop the pilot is satisfied that should the weather head for the cellar with no alternates near the destination, or something else occurs that requires the airplane to stay in the air longer than predicted, he or she has the fuel necessary to get to an airport where a safe landing can be made.

Experience in itself does not necessarily lead to professionalism.

Experience in itself does not necessarily lead to professionalism. A pilot with 5,000 hours of taking chances and bending the rules to his or her liking is probably not looked upon with favor by others who fly the straight and narrow. But as a person matures his or her attitudes ought to change as well. And that is the key to the whole subject of professionalism. Attitudes.

Our ATC system is designed around the professional pilot, and those who fail to display a reasonable amount of professionalism while operating within it will have problems. Amateurs in other fields seldom display the attitude that most pilots who do not fly for a living project. The system is not always easy to deal with, and in fact can be very frustrating at times. The workload it puts on the instrument pilot is significant, and one who flies a light aircraft without an autopilot in IFR conditions cannot afford to be haphazard or take chances.

Do you have to be an instrument pilot to display professionalism? Not at all. Any pilot, no matter what uses they have for an airplane, should consider the standards under which he or she operates. From those standards personal limits should be developed and everything the pilot does, from the preflight inspection to the securing of the airplane after the flight, must be with those ideals as the highest priority.

Where will the student pilot get his or her first inkling of professionalism? It might come from another pilot who provides an introduction to flying via a flight or flights before instruction begins. But usually the most significant element in developing standards for professionalism is the basic flight instructor. When the student pilot begins flight training usually he or she has little knowledge of the rules and the tasks a pilot faces before, during, and after a flight. The combination of the student's attitude and the instructor's devotion to safe operation is what eventually emerges in the new pilot as his or her level of professionalism.

Some students may feel there is something wrong with the instruction they are receiving, but most will not know the difference between good and bad unless they have pilot friends who perceive problems with the way the student seems to be heading in terms of the knowledge, or lack of it, the student displays for them at the various stages of training. Then, there are students who, no matter how good the instructor is, will not accept the correct doctrine and go their own way.

A student pilot was released by his instructor for his first solo flight in a Cessna 152. The instructor told him to fly the pattern three times, making full stop landings each time. On the third takeoff he departed the traffic pattern and did not acknowledge his instructor's attempts to call him on unicom. He proceeded to his daughter's house where his son-in-law took some pictures of the airplane as it flew by. A short time later the aircraft was seen flying very low over a golf course. Witnesses saw the aircraft enter a steep left bank before it disappeared below trees. It crashed in an adjacent field, killing the pilot.

Of course we don't know all that transpired between the student and instructor during the training, but in normal circumstances we would not expect a student on his or her first solo to act in that manner. Is it likely that the instructor failed to impress on the student the need for following instructions and not leaving the traffic pattern without permission? Probably not. The pilot's general attitude is likely to have impacted the decision to do what he did.

Some part of a pilot's professionalism has to come from life's non-flying events.

So, some part of the professionalism that one develops while learning to fly has to come to that person from life's other events. If he or she is not willing to play by the rules before learning to fly chances of an attitude change in an airplane are slim, but generally speaking if the instructor presents the student with a professional atmosphere that will probably be influence enough to get the message across.

The basic drive behind professionalism is excellence and the desire for it. An instrument pilot who strives for improved performance each time he or she flies will be one who exhibits professionalism. One who is satisfied with a mediocre performance leaves a lot to be desired and probably will not provide his or her passengers, or others who come into contact with the flight, with a satisfactory level of safety. Professionialism varies from pilot to pilot and operator to operator. But no matter the level of professionalism, excellence and the need for it remains the focal point. It is probably true that those who do not strive for professionalism in their flying do not strive for excellence in any part of their lives.

Professionlism is not exhibited by getting an airplane from point A to point B during hazardous conditions when no one else will accept the responsibility. A pilot who champions himself or herself after a flight of that magnitude should be avoided. It is just the opposite. A pilot who refuses to fly when conditions are not within their personal limits, or when there is some question about the ability of the airplane to perform under the circumstances, is the type of pilot to receive the accolades.

A good example is the decision to take off knowing that your alternate does not really meet the letter of the law. It is easy to rationalize that there is another airport only 10 miles from your original destination that has an ILS and that it is reporting the same weather and offers the same forecast as your destination. But the rules do not allow you to use an airport for an alternate unless it meets the legal criteria (see Chapter Eighteen). And in light singles and twins it is sometimes difficult to find an alternate that is within the range of the airplane's fuel supply. Does that mean you take off anyway? Not if you have a professional attitude toward what you are doing.

Marginal performance is not acceptable because minimum standards have been met.

Striving for excellence, hence professionalism, does not mean you will avoid mistakes along the way.

But the pilot who understands and accepts his or her role as a pilot based on those two precepts will work hard to keep the errors few, and when one is made will be quicker to realize and correct it. Remember that marginal performance is not acceptable simply because the minimum standards for your project have been met.

In spite of new technology, flying demands more and more of pilots with each passing day. High density airspace in particular can be a trial for any instrument pilot, especially if he or she is unfamiliar with the area. It is not that the physical act of flying the airplane is so difficult. It is not. But when you consider the individual tasks that an instrument pilot must perform, especially if flying solo during a single instrument flight, you cannot help but wonder at the workload. The pilot who strives for professionalism demands more from himself or herself and meets the challenge.

There are operators who would fire a pilot who exhibits "too much" professionalism in his or her work to always keep the airplanes moving and the money coming in. But more often than not the pilot is eager to go along. Why? Because the pilot wants to build time toward a better job, and any blemishes, such as being fired or branded as a troublemaker, can ruin that person's chances for the "good job." Pilots often call it "paying your dues," but setting professionalism aside temporarily while you search for the job of your dreams is not something you can do. It is tempting for a young, eager pilot to take any job that comes along, but the consequences of that action can bite hard. Some do not survive to take advantage of the money and benefits of that job that is just over the horizon.

If you are a pilot who is constantly seeking to better yourself, who knows what your limits are, and respects those of the airplane you fly, you have a good start on professionalism. But it is something we strive for all the time, not only on certain occaisions. Always strive for excellence and don't let honest mistakes worry you. It is the ones caused by a poor attitude that will kill you.

CHAPTER SEVEN

WEATHER BRIEFINGS

Instrument pilots have different attitudes about the weather and the type of weather briefing they receive. One pilot might check it continuously for several hours before a planned flight, while another would get a briefing a couple of hours before departure and be satisfied. Of course, how good or bad the weather is should directly influence amount of time spent looking at what a pilot can expect to find along the route of flight.

In the past the National Weather Service or Flight Service Station were the only sources of weather information for pilots. That has changed over the last

10 years or so. Now, while the Weather Service no longer normally accommodates pilots, there is good information available from The Weather Channel, Direct User Access Terminal (DUAT), Flight Service, and other pay-for-weather services. Which service or services you use or subscribe to will depend on your experience level and ability to read and interpret what you receive. Some pilots like having direct contact with a briefer, while others, usually those more experienced, prefer a complete self-briefing.

Whatever source you choose for your weather, you must think ahead. Flying on the gages takes much more planning than does a VFR flight if the outcome is to be successful. And you must know beforehand exactly what information is necessary to make the go/no-go decision. Making a decision not to go will not hurt you, but if you make the decision to begin a flight without all the weather facts in your possession you are likely to run into trouble.

The first thing to do after the destination is known is to pick a preferred alternate: an airport that you would like to use in the event you must legally file one. Then decide on your preferred fuel stop(s). Those should be easy tasks if you know your airplane well and have flown routine IFR flights in it in the past. If you are not sure about what is around the destination for alternates or where your fuel stop(s) should be it is best to plan your complete route before going any further, so you will be familiar with the destination area, the routing, and the airports along the way.

This should all be done days in advance of a known flight, or as far in advance of a pop-up flight as possible. The earlier this basic information is available to the pilot, the more of a handle he or she can get on weather forecasts for the time the flight is to take place. For example, I watch The Weather Channel up to five days in advance of a known flight to see how the weather systems are expected to move and to get an idea of how they might affect my flight. As flight time draws closer I am familiar with the major systems and what they might mean, how they have tracked across the country, and how they may continue to affect my route. The day before a flight I log onto DUAT and look at the route in more detail. The area forecasts and terminal forecasts issued 24 hours in advance of my departure give me an idea of what to expect at my originating airport, along the route, and at the destination. Those early forecasts help me decide whether the information I have been gathering over the last few days is correct, and in most cases I have a good idea at this point whether the flight will go as scheduled or not. If there is any question about whether I will fly the next day I make alternate arrangements at this point. Then, if it turns out that I cannot fly I have another way of getting where I need to go.

Alternate plans are a very important part of preflight activity.

Alternate plans are a very important part of your preflight activity. Too often pilots feel forced to begin a flight that they know is questionable, because of weather or other factors, because they don't have any other way of getting where they need to go. By having other plans ready the decision not to go, if everything is not exactly right, is much easier to make.

No matter how you get your weather you must know exactly what you want before picking up the phone or calling a service with your modem. Some pilots complain that the DUAT system gives too much information, much of which is discarded. But what you get is basically what the Flight Service briefer sees when he or she goes into the computer looking for the weather along your route. The briefer sorts it out and summarizes it for you. With DUAT you must do it for yourself. I think that many of those who complain about DUAT don't really know how to interpret the weather for themselves and would best be served by talking to a live briefer or learning more about the weather.

Safety of flight is the pilot's responsibility - not the weather briefer's.

When Flight Service weather briefers are busy they don't always give you all the information you need, and some pilots fail to ask for it. Accidents have been attributed in part to the briefer's failure to mention icing conditions, for example, and the pilot's complete neglect of the subject when he or she should have been aware that icing in the clouds could be a problem. Remember, safety of flight is the pilot's responsibility - not the weather briefer's. Let's look at an example of a flight that did not have a successful outcome because the pilot failed to get the information he needed.

The pilot called the Teterboro Flight Service Station for a briefing for a flight from Teterboro, New Jersey to Clintonville, Wisconsin. The plan was to fly his Aero Commander 680FLP back to his home base. The briefing contained a brief synopsis of the weather along the route plus forecasts. But the briefer did not mention anything about forecast icing, nor did the pilot ask about it. This was in the days before the FAA standardized the briefings that pilots receive. The Commander pilot filed an IFR flight plan for 12,000 feet, probably figuring he would be on top of everything. It appears that he was not concerned about icing.

The departure controller vectored the Commander toward the Solberg VOR and step-climbed the airplane to 10,000 feet, asking twice for a good rate of climb. Then the New York Center Controller cleared the aircraft to 12,000 feet and again asked for a good rate of climb, not an unusual request in a high density area. The pilot decided to stay at 10,000 feet and that request was granted, but shortly after arriving there he asked for 12,000 again. The controller told him it was not available but would be in about 10 miles. Before long the pilot asked to descend to 6,000 feet and was cleared to 8,000.

The Commander pilot was having problems with his navigation. The controller asked if he was proceeding along Victor 30 as cleared and the reply was, "We're navigating back to it." The requested changes in altitude and the aircraft's drifting off course indicate that the pilot was preoccupied with something else, probably ice that was building on the airframe. He acknowledged that he was having a problem when the controller advised him that it was not customary to change heading unless ATC approved. That was the last transmission from the aircraft.

The Commander crashed near Sunbury, Pennsylvania, about one hour after takeoff. Witnesses observed the airplane break out of the clouds with the nose nearly vertical and the airplane spinning to the left. The ceiling in the vicinity of the accident was said to be very low and "misty."

About an hour after the accident a retired airline pilot arrived on the scene. He reported to the NTSB that he observed clear ice, about a half inch thick, that conformed to the shape of the flying surface, lying on the ground under the leading edge of the stabilizer. The surface air temperature in the vicinity of the accident was 45 to 49 degrees.

There were several pilot reports of icing in the vicinity, one from a Beech 99 that indicated that while the de-ice boots cleared the wings the build-up on unprotected surfaces resulted in a rapid reduction of lift. We don't know where or at what altitude the ice began to accumulate on the Commander, but it was probably early in the climb. When the controller asked for a good climb rate, if the pilot pitched the nose up too high, he probably accumulated some ice low on the wings behind the leading edge. He may have asked to level off at 10,000 feet to build up airspeed that was decaying because of the load of ice he was carrying.

The pilot was not too concerned about ice because above 10,000 feet he thought he would be in the clear. He never got to clear air.

It appears that before the flight the pilot was not too concerned about ice because he was planning on climbing above 10,000 feet where he thought he would be in the clear. He never got to clear air. I don't know how much experience he had flying in high density airspace, but climbs and descents are not accomplished as fast as one would like under normal operating circumstances, as opposed to low traffic areas where the aircraft may be cleared up to the cruise altitude before it leaves the ground.

It appears that the pilot made a series of errors that began with a poor weather briefing and was compounded by his expectation that he would climb to his cruising altitude quickly. Also, he never said anything about having an icing problem before the controller queried him about being off course. By then it was probably too late to do anything.

Now you should understand why the weather briefing is so important. There are many weather-related reasons why a particular flight should not begin. Yet time after time we read about pilots who take off in the face of weather that is questionable for their experience level and the equipment they are flying. Most have been briefed properly and know about the weather, while others, like the Commander pilot, don't get the information they need to make a reasonable decision about flying that day.

After an accident occurs it is too late to go back and say to a pilot that he did not get a good briefing, or to a briefer that he failed to give the pilot enough information. Again, the safety of flight is up to the pilot, who must know what information is needed and ask for it if the briefer doesn't offer it.

Another problem you may run into while being briefed for a flight is that one specialist might tell you one thing and another, in a later briefing, tell you some-

thing completely different. Who's right? That is for
you to decide, and once again it points out the need for
the pilot to be adept at understanding the weather himself or herself.

My wife and I landed at Athens, Georgia for
fuel late one afternoon on the way to Lakeland, Florida
a couple of years ago and I called Flight Service for an
update on the weather. An earlier briefing had indicated the chance for scattered thundershowers in northern Florida during the day, and the briefer in Georgia
told me there was a solid line of thunderstorms from
Jacksonville to near Tampa. He claimed that the forecasts indicated it would be in the area all night. I
thought it odd that things had changed so much in a
couple of hours, but thunderstorms are hard to predict
accurately. I was wondering if we shouldn't stay in
Athens overnight when I walked into the lobby and spotted the radar on the Weather Channel. Sure enough,
there was a line over northern Florida but it was moving rapidly east. There was no question that by the
time we got to Lakeland that stuff would be off the
coast. There was nothing else behind it. I began to
wonder what radar that FSS briefer had been looking
at.

We took off and flew all the way to Lakeland
without any weather problems. After dark we saw the
lightning from the storms east of the shoreline, but we
had a good ride with hardly a bump and very few clouds.
As it turned out, had we not made it to Lakeland that
night it would have been mid-afternoon the next day
before we could have completed the trip because of a
thick ground fog that developed overnight and remained
until sometime after noon.

*A briefer can only tell you
for certain what is known,
such as pilot reports. Everything
else is an interpretation.*

That doesn't mean you should disregard anything a briefer tells you, but be aware that it is all a
matter of how individuals interpret the weather information they have in front of them. And the only things
a briefer can tell you for certain is what is known, such
as when a pilot reports there is ice in the clouds, or
severe turbulence, or when the briefer sees thunderstorms popping up on the radar display. Everything
else is a matter of an individual's interpretation. That
is why it is important that pilots have a good understanding of the weather and learn to interpret the reports themselves.

Forecasting the weather is difficult, and even
the experts are not always right. But if you are going
to do any serious instrument flying on a routine basis,
you should learn enough about the weather to make
good, reasonable decisions based on the information
you receive. Does that mean you have to be a professional forecaster? No, it doesn't.

What should you look for in a weather briefing? The FAA has three types of briefings available
for pilots who call or visit the Flight Service Station.
The first is the standard briefing, which is intended to
give you the entire weather picture. But if you are
flying to or from an area you are not familiar with when
the briefer reads the location of the weather systems
and how they are expected to travel during the course
of the day, it might not make any sense to you. A low

that is accompanied by a cold front in one direction and a warm front in another can be confusing when described over the phone, and the abbreviations for some of the locations in the DUAT text are just as bad. I usually watch the Weather Channel or another TV weather broadcast before calling Flight Service or DUAT. That way I have a good visual picture of the systems, and when the briefer or the area forecast summary describes their locations I have a better idea of what they are talking about.

After describing the systems the briefer will alert you to any hazards, like ice or thunderstorms, and tell you where the tops are forecast to be. He or she will probably stop right there if others have canceled because of the hazards. A briefer with many other pilots waiting on the phone would prefer to end the discussion and go on to the next call if you are not going to go.

If what you have been given so far is not enough for you to make a reasonable decision don't let the briefing end there. Tell the briefer that you need more information on the hazardous weather. Just because thunderstorms are forecast doesn't mean they will materialize. On my Lakeland trip, had I not had the input from the radar I probably would not have reached my destination that night.

You don't want to be out flying when conditions are more than you can handle, but you shouldn't cancel a flight prematurely without knowing all the details of the hazardous weather. Are there pilot reports verifying ice in the clouds or severe turbulence? Are the thunderstorms, or the conditions that will cause them to grow, beginning to develop?

The next item in the standard briefing will be the current weather conditions followed by the forecasts. This is where you probably want to be when you start thinking about the go/no-go decision. What is out there at the reporting stations along your route of flight, and what do the terminal aerodrome forecasts (TAF) look for? Are they accurate or have they been amended? A forecast that is on amendment three or four is useless. That means the forecaster has no idea what is going and is just chasing the current conditions.

If you cannot find your way around forecast freezing rain, your decision is made.

When freezing rain is forecast and it is being reported along the route, if you cannot find a way around it your decision is made. That's because freezing rain constitutes severe clear icing, and it will adhere to the entire airplane, causing aerodynamic problems with little build-up. But if the forecast is calling for clearing in the next couple of hours and it looks like you will have a straight shot at your destination you might want to delay an hour or so and see if the forecasts are right. Freezing rain is treacherous and a danger to all airplanes. More on that in Chapter Fifteen in the discussion of icing conditions.

If your destination doesn't report weather or have a TAF issued then the briefer will use the station(s) closest to it that do report. Depending on the distance from the station to that reporting or forecasting point, the weather in the two places could be different.

Ask if there is a way around any weather on the route that you don't want to deal with. How much of a routing change you can accept will depend on the type of airplane you are flying, the amount of fuel you can carry, and the availability of fuel along the way.

Finally, the briefer will read you the winds aloft and notices to airmen (NOTAMS). He or she might skip some enroute NOTAMS that could be important if you decided to land short of your destination. That is where DUAT is helpful because it gives you all the NOTAMS along the way, and you can have a printed copy to take with you. If you decide to change your destination you can look at your copy to see if there are any NOTAMS for your new destination or the area around it.

When you are finished is the time to make your decision unless conditions appeared to be so bad earlier in the process that you were sure to scrub the trip. If it is still a tossup hang up the phone and do whatever brainstorming is necessary. Are the hazards real? Can you get around them? Do you have enough fuel to make it to your destination and still have alternate fuel remaining? Are the alternates solid? Will the weather at the one you choose be suitable if you need to go there? What other options do you have for landing short of your destination, within the destination's terminal airspace, or within a reasonable distance from it? Remember, just because you have a legal alternate, that doesn't mean you have to go there if you cannot land at the original airport.

The second type of briefing available to pilots is the "abbreviated briefing." You should request that when you already have the basic information and need an update on any of the items that were covered. You should indicate to the briefer when you had your last briefing and what items you would like him or her to detail for you. If there are any adverse conditions forecast or reported along your route the briefer will advise you of those, and you should indicate whether you need current information on them or if you already have the latest update.

The "outlook briefing" is the last of the pre-flight briefings. If your proposed departure time is six hours or more away the briefer will give you a concise reading of what is forecast for your route. This briefing is intended to be used for planning only and does not relieve the pilot of the responsibility for getting a complete briefing before departure.

One thing to be careful of is the age of the forecasts you are dealing with. If they are within a couple of hours of expiring, you can look back and see what their track record was. If they were close to the actual conditions the forecasters have a handle on what is going on. If they were amended more than once you should wait for the new forecasts to come out. Be wary of forecasts that you think are just mirroring actual conditions. When forecasters are playing "catch-up," you should be prepared for anything.

The phrases "occasional" or "chance of" mean the forecaster is hedging bets.

A forecast for weather with visibilities greater than 3 miles is likely to be more accurate than one forecasting IFR conditions. That is because it is difficult for anyone to accurately predict low ceilings and visibilities when there are so many factors that can cause them to change. And that is why you usually see variables in the forecasts such as "occasional" or "chance of." Those two phrases are where the forecaster hedges his or her bets. It may make sense to the meteorologist, but the pilot who has to make decisions based on that information has a job cut out for him or her.

Years ago I was flying a Cessna 402 from Hilton Head, South Carolina to Providence, Rhode Island. I had planned to stop for fuel at Norfolk, Virginia. The forecasts indicated good VFR weather all the way up the coast. But as the sun set and light changed to dark, fog started developing everywhere. When I checked the ATIS at Norfolk the station was reporting below landing minimums. I called Flight Service and got the bad news. The only airports south of New York City still open were Atlantic City and Philadelphia. I did some calculations and decided I could make it to Atlantic City with an hour of fuel left in the tanks on landing. Philadelphia was forecast to be a suitable alternate.

Atlantic City remained VFR until just before I got there, then it went down quickly. Just as I passed the outer marker on the ILS approach the tower told me that the ceiling was 100 feet obscured, 1/4 mile visibility with a runway visual range (RVR) of 1,800. I did not descend into the stuff until I was about 800 feet above the ground, but it was thick. Fortunately I saw the approach lights when I looked up at minimums and followed them to the runway. A Twin Otter landed behind me, then the airport went below minimums. The Twin Otter captain wanted to go to Philadelphia, but it had gone down the tubes just before Atlantic City. So much for alternates.

So, it is important that you make the right decisions with the information you have before takeoff. Once you are airborne you need to stay abreast of what is going on and be prepared to change your destination or get on the ground quickly in the face of deteriorating weather. Don't take any chances with the weather while airborne. If you don't like what you are hearing you are better off to be on the ground checking the weather than airborne with no place to go. Conditions can change rapidly, as they did the night I was flying up the coast, and you must be prepared to deal with whatever happens.

Forecasts are not the gospel. They are what a human being thinks will happen. You should keep in mind that they may be wrong from the beginning and make your decisions accordingly. Remember, you want to get from your departure airport to your destination safely. That is the mission. Knowing and understanding the weather and how it relates to your flight will be what determines if you are successful or not.

CHAPTER EIGHT

END RUNNING THE WEATHER

The second briefer told me, "If you can get out of there in the next 30 minutes and head due north, you'll avoid the weather. If you don't make that, you'll be stuck for a while." "There" was Gaithersburg, Maryland, not far from Washington, D.C. My wife and I spent a few days visiting the nation's capital, and we were ready to head home. Back then we still had our 1957 Cessna 172 that had been completely restored and certified for IFR flight. I had called to update our weather briefing before getting into the airplane and calling for our clearance.

The early morning weather did not look good

for a direct flight back to the Detroit area. There were some heavy thunderstorms bearing down on Maryland from the west with more in the Pittsburgh area along a northeast-southwest cold front. To the north the weather was better though still IFR. There were low clouds in advance of the front but no thunderstorms yet near the Great Lakes, and only a chance of them forecast in the Cleveland area. After keeping the initial briefer on the phone for some time discussing alternate routes, I filed a flight plan to Buffalo, then another to our home base near Pontiac, Michigan.

There was one airplane ahead of us at the departure runway, and we waited about 10 minutes for our clearance to take off. We climbed into the fog at 500 feet and broke out on top of the clouds at 3,000 feet flying a northerly heading to avoid the weather. We could see it to the west, and the briefer was right. Had we been delayed much longer we would have been forced to return to the ramp and tie the airplane back down.

I checked the weather several times during the flight and changed our destination to Jamestown, New York when it became apparent that there was no severe weather north of the Pittsburgh area, nor did any appear to be developing. We flew a VOR approach and landed to refuel. Jamestown was 700 and 2.

Jamestown still had a small flight service station, and we visited it to get yet another review of the weather. The briefer was very helpful. Although he did not have real-time weather radar to show us, he plotted the radar summaries, and that showed us where the severe weather was. We would have had a clear shot along the southern coast of Lake Erie, but a few cells were starting to pop up along that route. To the north, over Canada, there was nothing. The Detroit area was on the other side of the front and was clearing rapidly.

I wanted to keep our exposure over Lake Erie to a minimum so I filed to the Dunkirk VOR, Aylmer VOR, and then along the northern coast of the Lake into the Detroit area. I knew that once we cleared the front we would be in VFR conditions.

Again, the tops were at 3,000 feet, and as we were crossing the lake heading toward Aylmer the clouds disappeared, and the rest of the trip was great. The air was clear, the visibility unlimited, and not a bump in the sky.

The front stalled later in the day when it was in reach of the coast, and had we delayed our flight until the next day we would have been stuck in Gaithersburg for at least three days. The coast got pounded with thunderstorms and heavy rains for most of that time. We got out in time, barely, but got home safely, and the ride, although longer than a direct routing would have been, was good.

Sometimes light airplane pilots have to be creative with their routings.

Sometimes light airplane pilots have to be creative with their routings in getting where they want to go. That flight was the result of a sharp Flight Service briefer who gave me the information I needed, then answered all my questions. I knew exactly what was happening. Then, while in flight, to prevent any

unforecast changes from causing problems that could
affect us without our knowledge, we kept in touch with
Flight Service by radio. Everything went as planned,
and the flight was successful.

By the way, I had a way out in case the weather
just to the west of Gaithersburg proved to be more of a
challenge to us than it was. I had a number of landing
choices, all to the north and east of Gaithersburg, and
had there been any indication that the severe weather
was building rapidly along our route north, or would
have prevented us from remaining clear of it, I would
have made a beeline for one of those airports.

I said earlier that flying instruments is a "head
game." And it is, no matter if the weather is low IFR
or marginal VFR. If you don't understand what the
weather is doing along your route and develop plans to
deal with it, the chances of your flight being successful
are reduced.

*The old say is that "any landing
you walk away from is a good
landing."*

What is a successful flight? The old saying that
"any landing you walk away from is a good landing"
implies that a crash landing, regardless of the reason
for it, is a good landing as long as the pilot and passengers are still mobile with few injuries to show for it. I
can conjure up visions of a Hollywood movie showing
the sensational crash landing of a private airplane of
some type, say a corporate jet. One engine is on fire,
the other is giving fits for unknown reasons. The pilots struggle with the controls and crash onto a runway

that just happens to appear out of nowhere. The wheels collapse and sparks ignite the Jet-A in the fuel tanks, engulfing the airplane in a fireball akin to a major disaster. But a few seconds later the pilots and passengers are shown observing the burning airplane from a distance making some inane comments about how good a landing it was.

But real life is different. Rarely is a crash landing of any kind considered a good landing. In fact, FAA enforcement records probably would show that many landings that would qualify under the "walkaway" good landing standard caused their pilots much legal grief. A successful instrument flight must also meet stricter criteria than survival.

A pilot who takes off into bad weather without knowing enough about what he or she faces may get to the destination in one piece, but will the flight be successful? I suppose it depends on your outlook. For example, some pilots plan their flights to the nth degree with a great deal of professionalism and take the time to learn exactly what the weather is doing and what can be expected from it. There is no doubt that it does not always do what is expected, but this type of pilot understands that and has alternate route plans and destinations in mind before he or she is willing to take off. If conditions are so bad that there are no alternatives, he or she does not go.

But there are others whose attitude toward the weather, and flying in general, is much different. I knew a number of pilots over the years who did not care what the weather was forecast to do. They were going to go anyway. Some of them are no longer with us, and a couple are no longer flying because their last flights were far from successful.

Too many pilots disregard the entire weather briefing and take off into severe weather, hard icing conditions, or knowing not only that there are no alternates available but that the destination forecast is shaky as well. If anyone were to plan an unsuccessful instrument flight it probably would be around such a scenario. Some pilots tell themselves they are going to have a look at what is out there, but in reality they are saying, "I'm going, no matter what."

So, the next time you are briefing for an instrument flight make sure your brain is engaged and the clutch is not slipping. Two basic questions need to be answered before you can make a reasonable go/no-go decision. If you are not willing to take the time to do the mental work why even bother with the briefing? You might as well just get in the airplane and go. During the flight you will find out if you were up to it or not.

The first question is fundamental to a successful flight. Are you certain that the current and forecast weather is within your capabilities? If you cannot answer an unqualified "yes" then delay the flight until conditions improve. If it is a marginal situation where it could go either way and you are inclined to launch, make sure you have a way out; an airport where the weather will be above that defined by your personal limits that is well within the fuel range of your airplane. It is helpful if you can find one or more airports along the route that you could land at if things head for the cellar quickly. But if there is no safe haven don't go.

While we are on the subject, do you know what

your personal limits are? Every pilot has them whether he or she realizes it or not. It is those who recognize them who plan successful flights. A good definition of a personal limit is, "the level somewhat below that of maximum competence where the pilot feels comfortable working a given task."

A personal limit should never be set at your maximum level of competence. You should always leave room in case something unexpected happens. For example, if you are barely comfortable doing instrument approaches when the ceiling is 400 feet make your personal limit 500 feet. Give yourself a buffer in case the weather does not do quite what you expect, or in case you experience a problem that requires some of your attention. Any distraction will rob some of your proficiency, especially if you are not at your performance peak, and it is difficult for most non-professional pilots who fly IFR to maintain themselves at their maximum skill level.

During your weather briefing if it appears that conditions will be within your skill level and meet your personal limits, you must then determine the reliability of the information you are receiving. How accurate have the forecasts been during the course of this system? Do the forecasters know what they are talking about or are they simply issuing forecasts based on current conditions?

There is other information that you must gather during the course of your briefing. If you are not going to be comfortable flying in the conditions you know are out there, and if you cannot have some faith in the forecasts, then the success of the flight is in doubt before it leaves the ground. If there is reason to doubt the outcome of the flight, there is reason to delay or cancel it. Pilots don't like to cancel flights, especially if there will be any negative feedback from passengers, but your established personal limits make it easier to do so should the need arise.

The first thing in your mind
each time you call for weather
is not necessarily what your
destination is doing.

If your decision is to go, once you are airborne you cannot relax and just allow things to happen. There is much more work to be done in addition to flying the airplane. You have to stay abreast of the weather conditions and whether they are meeting the forecasts or not. The first thing in your mind each time you call for weather is not necessarily what your destination is doing, but whether you still have places to go. That is the important thing. If you have landing sites available within a reasonable range of your present position, supportable by the amount of fuel in the tanks, then you have little to worry about unless some unexpected severe weather or icing is developing.

Remember too, that if you have to do an end run around some weather you don't want to deal with, it will eat into your fuel reserves. Depending on how much time it will add to the trip you might need to make a fuel stop. Don't allow yourself to put it off because you think you have the fuel to get where you are going. Your personal limits should include a minimum amount of fuel that you will land with or a minimun number of gallons required for continued flight, and if that amount is to be less than the specification, stop. It takes time to make the stop, but better to lose some time than have the engine(s) go silent on final approach.

Perhaps now, having read this far, you can understand that the mental processes required to fly an airplane in the clouds are considerable. When you couple all the "headwork" that needs to be done just to stay ahead of events with the brain power needed to physically fly on the gages, it should be easier for you to see why some pilots overextend themselves. And seldom do we consider that each of us has a limit to the amount of information we can process at any time.

There are times when you may be flying along under VFR when you run into weather and decide to get an IFR clearance to continue your flight. There is nothing wrong with doing that, and everything we have just discussed applies to picking up a clearance enroute. If you call for a clearance without knowing what lies ahead you may be putting your flight in jeopardy.

If you suspect there is IFR weather ahead call Flight Service and get briefed on it. You should be making routine weather checks even when you are flying VFR. Be certain you have places to go if you decide to continue, and file an IFR flight plan that you will pick up along the route. It is always easier to have a flight plan in the system with a route already specified. If you just pop up and ask a controller for a clearance, he or she will oblige you if not too busy to handle your flight, but it will take time to get all the details worked out. It increases the controller's workload as well as yours.

If you need to transition from VFR to IFR do it

as early as possible. If you see weather ahead, get briefed on it, get your flight plan filed, and get the clearance. Don't continue under VFR into IFR weather. Many pilots do that every year, and too many of those flights don't have a successful outcome. If a controller is too busy to handle your IFR flight make a 180-degree turn away from the weather and wait until he or she can get to you, or try to work out a location where you can pick up a clearance. Perhaps a controller in an adjacent sector has the time to take your flight, but make sure that you stay in VFR conditions until you receive an instrument clearance. If it is impossible to do that and the controllers cannot handle your flight you will have to declare an emergency to get a clearance. There will be more on getting clearances in the next chapter.

Success is based on your feelings for how things went.

Your job is to make sure your flight is successful. And success is measured not by the fact that you don't crash your airplane when you land. It is based on your feelings for how things went. Did the weather cooperate throughout or did you have to make decisions that you were not expecting? Did you have more than your established minimum amount of fuel in the tanks at touchdown? If not what happened to make you use the reserve fuel? Is there something you can do to prevent that from happening again?

If your anxiety level was high during the flight what caused it? Did it interfere with your flying? Could you have foreseen whatever it was that disturbed you?

Why didn't you?

How did your instrument approaches go? Did you make all your crossing altitudes? Did you keep the VOR or localizer needles centered? Were you able to stay on the final approach course of the NDB approach? Did you maintain your minimum descent altitude and not bust minimums? Did you see the airport at decision height or make a missed approach?

When you get out of your airplane you will know if the flight was successful or not. The answers to those questions and others will tell the story. If you have doubts about anything you did during the flight or feel uncomfortable for any reason talk to someone about it. Look up your instrument flight instructor or a friend who is knowledgeable about instrument flying. Don't let whatever is bothering you go without resolving it. If you do, the next flight might be less successful than the one you just completed.

CHAPTER NINE

OBTAINING CLEARANCES

You cannot go anywhere in the IFR system without a clearance. There are several ways of getting one and all involve the use of the telephone or aircraft radio. How you do it will depend on whether you are at a controlled or uncontrolled airport or already aloft in VFR conditions.

You must be prepared to copy a clearance. Always have a pencil and paper handy. Trying to memorize it as it is read to you is a mistake. It is too easy to forget transponder squawk codes, airway identifiers, or departure control frequencies that are included. And if the clearance is something entirely different from

what you are expecting you might miss the routing portion and have to ask the controller to repeat the whole
thing. If you are issued a departure heading to fly,
forget the heading and fly the wrong one, you could
cause a traffic conflict, as did the Cessna 182 pilot who
departed Charlotte, North Carolina on Runway 18 after being cleared to use Runway 36. He almost collided with an airliner that was landing on Runway 36.

     The easiest way to learn to copy a clearance is
to listen to an ATC facility. If you have a controlled
airport near you, monitor the clearance delivery or
ground control frequency. The frequencies for each
airport are listed in the Airport/Facilities Directory.
If the reception where you live is not adequate you might
have to spend some time at the airport listening and
watching the traffic.

     Always read back any clearance you receive.
That is verification for you and the controller that it is
understood. If you read it back incorrectly the controller will identify the parts that were wrong and reis-
sue them. If there is anything in the clearance that you
don't understand query the controller. He or she will
call ATC and resolve the question. If you take off
with a lingering question about a clearance it could
cause problems later in the flight. If you were to suffer a communications failure before resolving it you
might not have an effective clearance.

*It is always better to resolve
problems with the route before
taking off.*

     For example, you are cleared from Hartford,

Connecticut to Providence, Rhode Island via V58. If you accept that routing without checking it, when you get to the TRAIT intersection (see Figure 1) you will find that V58 does not go to Providence. The correct routing should be V58 TRAIT, V139 Providence. As long as you have communications you can ask the controller about the error in the route when you discover it, but if you lose communications what do you do? It is always better to resolve any problems with the route before taking off.

At some of the larger airports airlines receive their clearances by data links, so there is much less congestion on the clearance delivery frequency than there was in the past. But you will often hear airline crews who don't have the data link capability only read back their transponder squawk. They do that to reduce the "airtime" on the frequency. By reading back only the squawk the pilot confirms that he understands the routine clearance, allowing others more access to the controller. You can do the same thing at these airports, but it is not a good idea.

General aviation clearances are usually unique. Rarely are our flights scheduled like those of the airlines, and we fly to different destinations all the time. So, to be sure that you understand the clearance it is always better to read it back in its entirety. It is your responsibility to understand the clearance, and if you copy it wrong and don't read it back it will become an issue at some point along the flight. If a traffic conflict is the result you will likely be hearing from the FAA.

At a controlled airport there is nothing difficult about contacting clearance delivery, ground control,

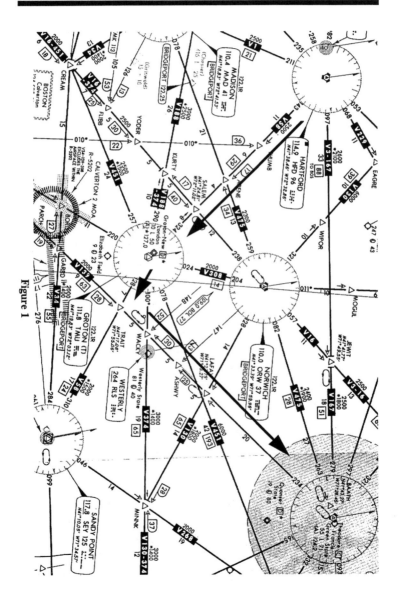

Figure 1

or whoever has the responsibility for issuing clearances. Some of the smaller controlled airports don't have a separate clearance delivery frequency, and you can identify the correct frequency to use for receiving a clearance by looking in your NOS approach plates or Jepps.

If you filed direct to a destination from a high density airport there could be a delay in getting your clearance. The controller will have to route you over a departure fix that might be a VOR or an intersection. These are usually identified in standard instrument departures (SIDs) or IFR area navigation charts. When I first started flying IFR, if a pilot filed direct to a destination it usually meant he or she was too lazy to do the correct flight planning and would take whatever routing ATC assigned. But today, with long range navigation readily available in many aircraft, filing direct in a flight plan is rapidly becoming commonplace. But it is doubtful that you will get direct routing out of a high density airport, so be prepared for an outbound fix. If there is a SID for the direction you are going, you can probably identify the fix ahead of time and put it in your flight plan. It could save some time.

If you are flying from one high-density airport to another you probably will be issued a clearance that includes a preferred route. These are routes that ATC commonly uses for controlling the traffic flow between city pairs. There are high-altitude and low-altitude preferred routes. They may be found in the Airport/Facilities Directory or in your Jepps. If a preferred route exists for the cities you will be flying between that is probably the routing you will be assigned, no matter what you filed.

But beware of preferred routings. Some, on the

east or west coast, for instance, might take you over water. If you are planning a trip in an airplane you would prefer not to fly over water put "no overwater routes" in the remarks section of your flight plan. But make sure you check the route you are issued before accepting it. If you don't understand what you have been issued and begin the flight, when you finally discover where it will take you getting it changed may be difficult. Sometimes the note in the flight plan is ignored and the clearance includes an overwater route. So, be careful about checking routing before accepting a clearance.

Some preferred routes are not published. They are the result of what the FAA calls "letters of agreement" between ATC facilities. For example, leaving the Detroit area southbound toward Dayton (see Figure 2) you will be cleared via "radar vectors to the Score Intersection, the DXO (Detroit VOR) 184-degree radial to intercept the FDY (Findlay VOR) 031-degree radial to FDY direct ROD (Rosewood VOR) Direct." That route is a a result of a letter of agreement between Detroit Approach Control and Toledo Approach Control on how the traffic will flow between the two facilities. How do you know that is what you will get? If you are not familiar with that routing in advance you will not know about it.

That is frustrating for someone who files direct to the Waterville VOR, which is near the Toledo Express Airport and some distance west of Score, then direct to Rosewood, and on to the destination. On the charts that route looks like it would be sensible and one you could expect to get. It can take 20 minutes extra for me to fly the route over Score and Findlay in

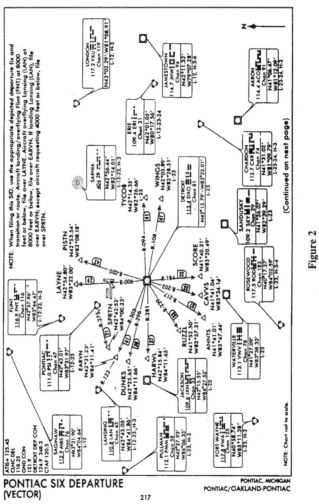

Figure 2
Not For Navigation

my Piper Arrow, depending on which Detroit area airport I depart from and the direction of the winds aloft. Someone who is not familiar with that routing, who accepts the clearance without checking, might be jeopardizing his or her alternate flight planning and onboard fuel reserves. Those routes should be published so pilots can plan for them.

Once you accept a clearance you are responsible for flying the assigned routing. ATC may issue amended clearances along the way, and you may request an amended clearance, though the density of the traffic will be the deciding factor in getting an approval for a new route.

*It is easy to mistake the name
of an intersection.*

Technically, each time a controller gives you a heading to fly he or she is amending your clearance. You must be alert for any instructions that are issued and acknowledge them. If you don't understand what you are being told ask the controller to repeat or clarify what he or she told you. With five-letter identifiers being used for intersections it is easy to mistake the name of an intersection being issued in a clearance because there are few vowels in them. If you are not sure what the intersection is ask the controller to spell it out for you, locate it on the chart, then read it back. There have been cases where pilots thought they understood the name of an intersection, put the wrong one in their GPS or Loran, and navigated in the wrong direction. That kind of mistake often leads to traffic conflicts, so be sure you understand the names and spelling of any intersections you are assigned in a clearance.

At controlled airports you call clearance delivery or ground control for your clearance, but at uncontrolled airports getting a clearance can be difficult and time-consuming. The easiest way to get a clearance is via a "remote communications outlet." That is where the local ATC facility has an antenna on the airport, or very close to it, and can communicate directly with pilots on the ground. Receiving a clearance via a remote communications outlet is not much different from getting it from clearance delivery at a controlled airport, except you may be issued a clearance void time. Airports that have remote communications outlets are identified by the "clearance delivery" frequency listed in the communications section of the approach plates for that facility.

When you call for a clearance at an uncontrolled airport a block of airspace is reserved for your flight. No other IFR airplanes are allowed into it until you are off the ground and have been identified on radar. After that the controller can maintain radar separation. But until he or she sees you on the scope it is your airspace. To avoid tying up the airspace for extended periods while an IFR airplane departs an uncontrolled airport, the airplane is usually issued a clearance void time. After the time specified in the clearance you may not take off.

Say you call for your clearance as you taxi out and the controller at the remote facility issues it to you. At the very end he or she will say, "clearance void at 10:33. Time now 10:28." That means you have five minutes to get off the ground.

You do your runup and taxi onto the runway. But as the power comes up you notice a problem with the manifold pressure and abort the takeoff. It is apparent to you that you will not make it off by 10:33, so you call to advise the controller. Should your runup take longer than you expect and you are not ready in five minutes you cannot take off. You call the controller and ask for a new void time.

How does the controller know how much time you need to get off the ground? He or she will ask when you call for the initial clearance. If you say you need ten minutes the window will be 10 minutes if other traffic in the area permits. If there is an inbound aircraft the controller might not have 10 minutes to give you, and probably will ask you if you can make it off sooner. If you cannot you will have to wait for the other aircraft to land before you get your clearance.

Another way of handling clearances from uncontrolled airports is to issue a clearance valid time and a clearance void time. If, for example, you tell the controller that you need ten minutes to get ready he or she might say, "clearance is valid at 10:33. Clearance is void at 10:36. Notify me if you don't become airborne by 10:39. Time now is 10:23." When the clearance is issued with a clearance valid time the airport and airspace are only tied up for three minutes, and you still get the 10 minutes to get ready to fly.

*You may be issued a clearance
with the tag "hold for release."*

You may also be issued a clearance with the tag "hold for release." That means that for whatever reason the controller cannot block the airspace for you yet. He or she may check to see what other IFR traffic is doing in the vicinity of the airport you are departing from, or get an okay to release you from another controller who is handling the airspace sector you are in. Or, there may be another airplane on the approach to the same airport and a valid or void time will not be issued until that airplane is on the ground.

It works the same way at airports that don't have remote communications outlets, except you have to call ATC on the telephone, either directly or through the local Flight Service Station. That makes it more complicated because you cannot talk to the controller once you hang up the phone. If you don't get off on time you have to taxi back to the ramp, make another phone call, explain why you did not get off, and get another clearance if you still want to go. Cellular telephones are great aids for pilots on the ground trying to get clearances because you can do your runup, then make the call and tell the controller you are ready to go. But don't use a cellular phone in the air except in an emergency such as a total communications failure. At some airports you can communicate with Flight Service by radio while on the ground, and that cuts out the need to get out of the airplane to make a phone call.

It is not likely that you will be given a "hold for release" clearance over the telephone. Usually if you call Flight Service for a clearance you will be issued the clearance or told to call back in a given amount of time. That way there is no confusion about a clearance being issued and an airplane taking off without the proper authorization.

If you call Flight Service for your clearance on

the ground and intend to get weather as well as your authorization to take off, get your weather first then have the briefer get your clearance. If you get your clearance first then ask for the weather, whatever time it takes for the briefer to get the data together and read it to you comes off your preparation time. If you had ten minutes to get airborne and you use three or four of it getting weather you may run out of time before you are ready to take off, or you may rush and forget something important on the checklist that will cause a problem during or after takeoff.

When you call Flight Service for a clearance or if you receive a clearance from a non-federal control tower, it will be prefaced with the words "ATC clears ... ." That means the clearance is coming to you via a third party who is relaying it for the appropriate facility. It is important that you understand the clearance completely before departing, and if you have any questions ask the person who reads it to you to answer them. He or she will have to call back to the facility that issued the clearance, but it is much safer to wait on the ground while a possible routing error is corrected than to launch with a routing that might cause a traffic conflict. The chances for error in a clearance increase with the number of people who handle it.

When it is VFR, pilots flying from uncontrolled airports, especially those that don't have remote communications outlets, take off and get their clearances in the air. A VFR departure saves time and the hassle of getting the clearance on the ground, but the pilot has to know two things before doing it. First, he or she must know that the weather will allow a climb in VFR conditions to a point where radio communications can be established with the controlling facility for the area. That means the airplane must remain in VFR conditions for whatever length of time it takes to get an instrument clearance. If there is any question about the ceiling and visibility get the clearance on the ground.

I generally use a minimum of 2,500 feet above ground level (AGL) in most areas where communications is not a problem, though there are a few areas where I can do with less, but not much less. In high terrain or mountains it might be necessary to have a higher ceiling that will allow you to clear terrain and reach the ATC facility that can give you the clearance you are seeking.

The pilot taking off VFR must be familiar with the terrain.

Second, the pilot must be familiar with the terrain he or she is taking off into. Crews of aircraft that only fly on instruments don't usually have VFR charts available. The only time they fly VFR is when they take off from an uncontrolled airport intending to get their clearance in the air. Here is a case in point.

A corporate BeechJet 400 was taking a group of executives on a tour of some of the company's facilities in different cities. They were scheduled to leave Rome, Georgia for Huntsville, Alabama at 9:30 one December morning. The Captain filed an IFR flight plan for the short flight to Huntsville, and when his passengers returned he decided to take off and get his instrument clearance in the air. The weather at Rome was only slightly better than basic VFR with a ceiling at 1,000 feet and 10 miles visibility. The information we have detailing the events in the cockpit before the accident is from transcripts of the cockpit voice recorder.

The first officer was flying the aircraft when it departed Rome, and the Captain called Atlanta Center for his clearance immediately after takeoff. The center controller advised him that there were two other airplanes on the approach to the airport, and that he would not be able to issue a clearance for a while.

The Captain was familiar with the area and knew there was high terrain nearby, so he told the first officer to make a 360-degree turn. Then he said, "We are going to have to get away from that mountain down there pretty soon." The Captain suggested a right turn, then he expressed concern about that direction because of the airplanes on approach to the airport, the mountain, and an antenna that he knew was nearby.

The first officer offered to "punch" the aircraft up through the clouds, but the Captain did not want to do that for fear of hitting the approaching aircraft. A short time later the aircraft struck the mountain at the 1,580-foot level, killing the nine people on board the aircraft.

Had the crew called for a clearance on the ground they would have been informed of the two inbound aircraft and told to wait for their clearance. The weather was VFR and the captain had the legal right to take off, but was it very smart? A thousand feet is not much of a ceiling for a turbine powered airplane that moves along at a rapid speed even that close to the ground. In fact, about the only thing you would want to do with a 1,000-foot ceiling is fly the traffic pattern, and that only in a light airplane. And just because the ceiling is 1,000 feet at the airport doesn't mean it is that high in adjacent areas.

Is delaying a flight worth it to avoid the risk of colliding with terrain that you cannot see? Obviously it is. Here is another tragic example.

The Hawker Captain called San Diego Flight Service Station three times in an hour-and-fifteen-minute period trying to figure out how he should depart Brown Field VFR and pick up his IFR clearance in the air. He had two problems. One was to stay clear of the San Diego Class B airspace, and the other was to avoid the mountains to the north and east of the airport.

The control tower at Brown had closed for the night, and during the first call to the FSS the briefer advised the pilot that he could get the clearance on the ground either by radio or telephone. The pilot said he would prefer to depart VFR and get the clearance in the air, probably because he did not want to keep his passengers waiting while the clearance came through. The airplane was scheduled to depart sometime after midnight, and at that time getting the clearance on the ground should not have resulted in any lengthy delays.

In the subsequent calls the pilot asked for guidance on how he should depart under VFR and stay clear of the terminal control area (TCA), now called Class B Airspace. At one point the briefer read the pilot the published IFR departure procedure for the airport, but the Captain was worried about a TCA infringement if he used it. Finally he decided that he could stay low, "say, down below 3,000" feet and fly northeast until he could get the clearance. The response from the briefer was, "Uh-huh."

That was not enough for the pilot so he asked, "Do you agree on that?" The briefer replied, "Yeah, sure, that will be fine."

The airplane hit Otay Mountain 170 feet below its summit while the pilot was waiting for an instrument clearance.

With that tacit approval of his proposed routing out of Brown Field the pilot loaded his passengers, fired up the Hawker's engines, and took off. Radar tapes showed that the airplane turned to and flew a 050-degree heading until it hit Otay Mountain 170 feet below its 3,300-foot summit. The pilot was waiting for an instrument clearance at the time.

So, when you decide to take off VFR and get your clearance in the air, you must know exactly what you are doing. Check the airport's approach plate for the minimum sector altitude that will provide you with information on safe altitudes within 25 miles of a nearby fix. Study any IFR departure procedures for the airport. If you follow the one for the runway you will depart, it should keep you clear of terrain, but if the clouds are too low to allow you to do that visually, get your clearance on the ground. The Hawker pilot was confronted with departure procedures that would have taken him into the San Diego Class B airspace, which would have been fine had he obtained an IFR clearance before takeoff. Check the procedures to be certain you will not be violating anyone's airspace if you elect to fly the departure procedure VFR.

For safety's sake get your clearance on the

ground whenever possible. If you elect to depart VFR and get it in the air, be certain you know what kind of terrain is in the area and that you can remain clear of it until you receive your clearance. Also, when you do get your clearance, be sure you understand it, and if you have any questions about it get them answered right away.

It is also possible to pick up a clearance in the air or on the ground when you don't have a flight plan filed. A "tower enroute" flight is one that usually can be flown within one controlling agency's airspace or between the boundaries of adjacent co-operating agencies. If you don't have a flight plan on file you may ask ground control or clearance delivery at your departure airport for a tower enroute clearance to your destination. The controller will put a flight plan into the system for you and issue you a normal IFR clearance. But beware of tower enroute. The pilot-in-command is still responsible for flight planning, receiving a weather briefing, and filing an appropriate alternate if necessary.

Since you did not file a flight plan with Flight Service you don't have an alternate listed with them. If one is required ask the controller who issues your clearance to enter your alternate airport in the remarks section of the flight plan he entered into the system.

Before calling for a clearance,
have a route ready to give to
the controller.

If you are flying VFR and find yourself needing an IFR clearance because of weather conditions in front of you, the ATC controller whose airspace you are in has the option of issuing one or not, depending on his or her workload. Before calling for the clearance you should have a route ready to give to the controller. That will reduce the time it takes him or her to issue the clearance. But you are still responsible for the pre-flight planning that would apply had you departed IFR and for filing an alternate if required. Again, you can ask the controller to place your alternate in the remarks section of the flight plan.

Some pilots don't know how to pick up an IFR clearance when airborne. Whether you have a flight plan on file or not you must know who to call for the clearance. That requires an understanding of how the ATC system operates and who is responsible for what airspace. A controller cannot issue you a clearance if you are in someone else's airspace.

When you depart an airport VFR intending to get the clearance as soon as you can talk to the local controller, you consult the instrument approach plate for the airport to find the local controlling agency and the frequency to use to contact ATC (see Figure 3). When you are enroute, though, the issue is a little more complicated.

Flight Service may help to determine whose air-

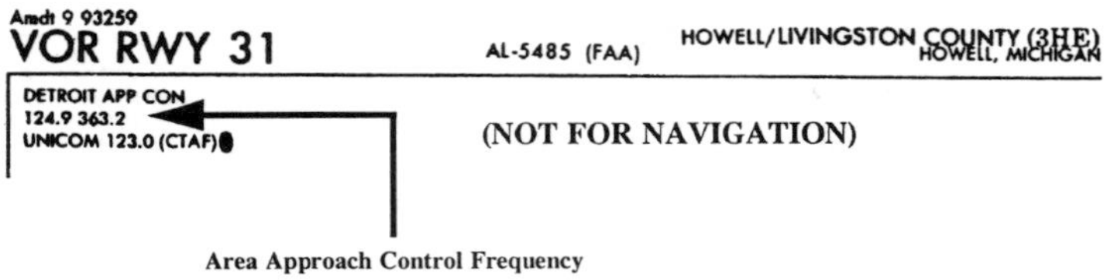

Amdt 9 93259
VOR RWY 31 AL-5485 (FAA) HOWELL/LIVINGSTON COUNTY (3HE) HOWELL, MICHIGAN

DETROIT APP CON
124.9 363.2
UNICOM 123.0 (CTAF) (NOT FOR NAVIGATION)

Area Approach Control Frequency

Figure 3

space you are in once you provide your position and altitude. The specialist probably will provide you with a contact frequency.

Another method of finding the right person to talk to is to consult your IFR enroute chart for the area you are flying through. Air Traffic Control Center frequencies are placed throughout the chart, designating different enroute sectors (see Figure 4). Calling the nearest center frequency and advising the controller of your position and altitude should also work. If you are not on the right frequency he or she will give you another to try.

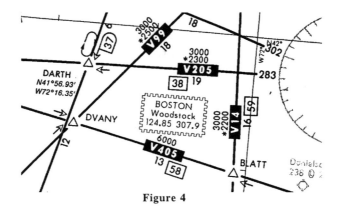

Figure 4

There is nothing difficult about picking up a clearance in the air once you are talking to the proper controller. Tell him or her where you are, your altitude, and that you would like to pick up a clearance to your destination. If you don't have a flight plan on file you will save time by mentioning that. Then pass along your proposed route and the controller will likely tell you to stand by while putting your request into the system. Be ready to copy your clearance on paper when the controller calls you back.

The ATC system, as complex and intimidating as it sometimes can be, works well when pilots understand how to operate within it. Some pilots are afraid of it and their anxiety is obvious when you hear them on the radio. More exposure to the system and some tutoring by a flight instructor or knowledgeable pilot will normally reduce any inhibitions one has about using ATC.

CHAPTER TEN

COMMUNICATIONS

Communicating is a large part of our lives whether we realize it or not. Some of us know how to do it better than others and have more success in our everyday endeavors. The same is true for communicating while flying.

If an instrument pilot does not know how to communicate with ATC he or she will have a tough time in the system. Flying the airplane is hard enough when you are in the clouds, but poor communications skills that cause more anxieties between a pilot and the ATC controller will make the job that much more difficult. And if you happen to be in a high-density area at "rush hour" and have problems understanding what a controller wants you to do, you could cause problems for other pilots as well as yourself and ATC.

Most pilots who have problems communicating with ATC cause the problem themselves. That is because they refuse to devote the time necessary to learn the proper procedures or phraseology. Sometimes they understand what they are supposed to do or say but decide to use other terminology because it sounds "macho" or more "professional" to their way of thinking.

Whatever the case, poor communications can result in traffic conflicts and accidents. A simple thing like missing a call from ATC because you are chatting with your buddy in the right seat, or another passenger, can cause traffic problems. Part of learning to communicate effectively is paying attention to the radio at all times and listening to others as well as calls from ATC for your flight. If you want to talk to your seatmate or listen to the Grateful Dead on CD-ROM or a talk show on the ADF, don't file IFR. Restrict your flying to VFR days.

When I started flying instruments, lightweight headsets were just coming on the market. When I bought my first one and started using it I could not believe how much easier it made flying in the clouds. I no longer had to reach for the microphone every time I needed to reply to rapid-fire ATC instructions. It was particularly helpful on instrument approaches because I could continue flying the airplane with both hands while acknowledging clearances. Today most pilots use headsets not only for the ease of operation they offer but for noise protection as well. It is probably the most valuable tool in the pilot's flight kit and makes the job of communicating with ATC so much easier.

If you are unfamiliar with the terminology that should be used between pilots and controllers check out the Aeronautical Information Manual (AIM). It has a whole chapter on communications phraseology and procedures plus a pilot/controller glossary in the back. There are valuable suggestions on techniques you should use and contact strategies. After reviewing that, take a scanner or hand-held radio and listen to ATC communications at a nearby airport that has a control tower. If reception is poor where you are, you can take a portable aviation band radio to the airport and watch the airplanes while you listen to the procedures they are using. Pay particular attention to the activity on the clearance delivery frequency if the airport has one. If it does not, clearances will be read over the ground control frequency.

Communicating over a radio and speaking into a microphone should be conducted in the manner of normal conversation.

Some people have what is called "mike fright." That is when the microphone intimidates them and they are afraid to speak into one. Some are so bad that they freeze and cannot say anything, while others chop their sentences into unrecognizable groups of words. In reality communicating over a radio, and speaking into a microphone, are nothing difficult and should be conducted in the manner of normal conversation.

While a pilot is working on his or her instrument rating he or she should be flying enough that talking over the radio becomes natural. The hardest thing to learn is to know exactly what you want to say to a controller. Tell him or her what you want as though you were in his or her presence. If you don't have the jargon right the first time it will come with experience. Speak naturally and in normal tones of voice. It is not necessary to scream into a microphone, nor should a pilot speak softly so his or her voice has what many consider "professional quality." The low-pitched tones that these pilots use to sound like "Mr. Cool" are often difficult to hear on the other end and cause problems for controllers and other pilots.

In reality talking via the radio is little different than talking to someone on the telephone. But our conversations over aircraft radios are more structured, and we are trying to get certain information to the controller while he or she is doing the same with us. Each transmission must be clear and concise, and words that convey exact meaning must be used if each party is to understand the other. That is why certain phrases and the techniques outlined in the AIM were developed.

Here is an example of a confusing statement. "Fort Worth Center, Skyplodder 1234 Golf, level 8,000." That probably does not seem too difficult to understand as you read the words on paper, but over a radio channel it is different. The problem is the word 'level.' When that word is received it can be confused with the word "leaving." In fact, that happened years ago over Long Island when two Boeing 747s were placed in the same holding pattern after a controller thought one of the pilots said he was "leaving" 13,000 feet. The controller was busy with many holding airplanes in his sector and thought the airplane had vacated that altitude, so he told another to descend to it. The weather was IFR and fortunately the mistake was discovered before the two airplanes got too close to each other. The word I use for reporting my altitude is "maintaining." That eliminates the confusion between "leaving" and "leveling" because the are so different.

Too many pilots don't follow the recommendations in the AIM, and when that happens communication suffers because the transmissions take too long and tie up the frequency unnecessarily, in addition to causing messages to be harder to understand (which also wastes time used for clarification). When a controller has to repeat an instruction or does not understand what you are telling him or her other important communications cannot be made. So, strive to make your transmissions as short as possible while getting your message across clearly.

Often misunderstandings between pilots and controllers during flight begin with clearance delivery. Five-letter designators for intersection names are confusing. If you have any question about one of those, whether it is on clearance delivery or in an amended clearance you receive while airborne, make sure you spell it back to the controller or ask him or her to spell it out for you. If you put the wrong ID into your Loran or GPS data base you could wind up flying in a direction different from what the controller intended. That could cause a traffic conflict. If you are issued a particular intersection that is unfamiliar and fail to verify its correct spelling you could be setting yourself up for trouble later in the flight.

Pilots often expect to hear
something and copy what they
expect rather than what is said.

But often, when receiving a clearance, pilots expect to hear something and copy what they expect rather than what is said. That is why it is important to read back your clearance for verification. A simple thing like an incorrect airway number can be confusing and cause hazardous situations later in the flight.

Awareness of what one is doing is what will prevent communications mishaps. If you are alert for radio transmissions for your aircraft you are halfway there. One problem is that other cockpit duties may divert your attention away from the radio, and a controller may give you a clearance that you don't even hear. If you don't understand that the transmission is for you the controller will have to call you until he or she gets your attention then repeat the clearance when you finally answer. Headsets help with communications awareness, but you have to be listening to the radio chatter to hear your callsign. Talking with a passenger may prevent you from doing that.

Some pilots turn the radio volume down so they can chat with a passenger over the intercom. Of course, both the intercom and the radio play into his or her headset. That might make conversation easier, but with the radio volume below that of the intercom the pilot is missing the communications that take place between the controller and other aircraft that could have a bearing on the flight, plus those intended for his or her aircraft.

How fast you speak on the radio is very important when communicating with others. If you talk too fast the controller probably will not understand you, and if the controller does the same you will not understand him or her. I remember one controller who worked in the tower at Providence, Rhode Island years ago, who spoke too fast. It did not matter what position he manned, he rattled his clearances off faster than most pilots could understand him. He probably had to repeat more instructions than any other controller I have ever run across. After a while I got used to him and could understand what he was saying, but many pilots, especially transients who seldom visited Providence, did not.

This controller was a private pilot and rented airplanes at a local FBO. More than once I observed him in conversation with other pilots, several of whom did not hesitate to tell him that he needed to slow down when talking on the radio. But he spoke at the same rate in person, and there was no slowing him down. Until the day he retired he spoke too fast on the radio.

Some pilots do the same thing. They speak so fast the controller does not understand what they are saying. If you have a weak radio or a bad microphone it is even more difficult to understand your words.

While you want to keep transmissions as short as possible, rushing will have the opposite effect.

If we are in a position where we expect to hear a certain thing, hear a quick burst of words that we think are what we anticipated, and act on that clearance without really understanding that it was not what we thought, a traffic conflict may be the result. The example of "level" or "leaving" is typical of that. Keep the speed of your transmissions at a pace so that anyone who hears you can understand what you are saying. While you want to keep your transmissions as short as possible, rushing your words will have the opposite effect because the statement will have to be repeated - or, worse, it may be misinterpreted.

I recently read an accident report where a controller at St. Louis was working seven different frequencies when an accident occurred because an airplane taxied into position on the wrong runway. While that controller probably should not have had that much responsibility, it is not uncommon in many ATC facilities for one person to be monitoring more than one frequency. For example, often controllers at low-density towers tell me to taxi into the ramp and monitor ground control. While listening to the ground control frequency I hear the same controller give an IFR clearance to an airplane on the clearance delivery frequency and give other aircraft taxi instructions on ground. He transmits on all the frequencies he is working simultaneously, so while he is transmitting on one frequency a pilot will not attempt to transmit to him on another. I have also heard approach controllers who were working approach and departure controls, tower, ground, and clearance delivery all at the same time. This usually occurs at night or very early in the morning when there is little traffic. You can see why it is important to keep our transmissions short and clear while using words that are easily recognizable.

Now let's get into some specifics regarding communications procedures. First is the initial call-up.

There are two things that are extremely important on the first call to an ATC station. You must identify whom you are calling and tell the controller who you are. There are some other required phrases depending on the phase of flight you are in. For example, if you are switching from one radar controller to another your transmission should be similar to this: "Cleveland Center, Skyplodder 1234 Golf, maintaining 6,000."

In most domestic communications the "N" in the callsign is dropped in favor of the aircraft type. In this example you are calling Cleveland Center, your aircraft type is a Skyplodder, and the callsign is 1234 Golf. You always give your altitude when you are IFR and signing on to a new frequency. That requirement goes back to the early IFR days when a controller, who did not have radar, wanted to verify what altitude the airplane was at on the initial call-up. Today it is used for the same purpose, but the controller is verifying the altitude he expects you to be at against that reported by your altitude encoder to be certain they are the same. Of course, if you are flying in an area where an encoding altimeter is not required and you don't have one, or yours fails during the flight, the controller is still getting the verification he or she needs when you tell him what altitude you are at.

Another example of an initial call-up would be the one immediately after release from the control tower on an IFR departure. You should say something like this: "Boston Departure, Skyplodder 1234 Golf is out of 1,500 climbing to 3,000." The elements are exactly the same as the enroute contact, and again the altitude report is used for verification that your encoder is working properly, and that you and the controller understand what altitude you have been cleared to.

*The initial call-up is very
imporant. It establishes contact
with a new controller.*

The initial call-up is very important because it establishes contact between you and a new controller. If he or she does not understand anything you say because you are speaking too fast or using words that don't make much sense, or your radio is garbled, it could lead to the conflicts I mentioned. If your callsign (N number) is similar to another one already in use on the frequency the controller might become confused and think it was the other aircraft that called. That can be troublesome on any frequency but especially so on clearance delivery.

If the clearance controller confuses your identification with another airplane he or she could read you the wrong clearance. You can correct that by giving him or her your correct ID, but time will be wasted on the frequency while the improper clearance is read. That delays everyone. And on the off chance that you happen to be going to the same airport as the other aircraft, major confusion could result.

So, your initial call to clearance delivery should be like this: "Dulles Clearance, Skyplodder 1234 Golf, instruments to Cleveland's Burke Lakefront with information Romeo."

Each of these sample transmissions gets the necessary information across to the controller while keeping the number of words and the amount of time the frequency is tied up to a minimum. Pilots who give their entire life stories to each controller they talk to are needlessly interfering with safety by keeping others, including the controller, from making important transmissions.

After the initial call-up the rules relax somewhat. The AIM says that if the controller uses an abbreviated callsign to identify your flight after the initial call-up, you can use that as well. For example, if the controller replies to you saying, "Skyplodder 34 Golf, radar contact, maintain 6,000," you can use the callsign "Skyplodder 34 Golf" the rest of the time you are on that controller's frequency. But situational awareness requires that you listen carefully to other transmissions for aircraft with numbers similar to yours. You don't want to accept a transmission for another aircraft, nor do you want to miss a transmission for your own.

Usually controllers tell you when an aircraft with a similar callsign is coming on the frequency. That is your cue to listen up for traffic for your flight. But sometimes a controller forgets to give the advisory, especially if he or she is busy. Occasionally a controller may not think a particular callsign is similar to yours, but when you hear it you want to respond. When I know there is another aircraft with a similar sounding callsign on the same frequency I use my entire callsign on every transmission I make, and I emphasize the type of aircraft (Skyplodder), so if the controller misses the N number for some reason he or she will catch the difference in types.

All transmissions should be acknowledged with the aircraft's callsign. That is the only way a controller will know that you received the clearance or other information that he or she sent. Simply saying "roger" after a transmission is made to your aircraft is not an acknowledgment, though you hear that used often by professional and non-professional pilots alike. If your callsign is not included in your reply the controller does not know who responded to the transmission, but may assume - perhaps erroneously - it was the correct aircraft. Another very bad habit is clicking the microphone to acknowledge transmissions. There is no way a controller can know that transmission came from your airplane.

I know a pilot who was charged with an altitude violation because he descended from 7,000 to 5,000 feet on a clearance that was meant for someone else. He acknowledged the clearance before he began the descent, but if he used the correct callsign the controller did not hear it.

Controllers not answering calls has been an issue for me.

Through the years, controllers not answering calls has been an issue for me. I have visited some ATC facilities and I know that when the traffic is heavy controllers have as much going on in their environment as the pilot in the cockpit. Attention may be distracted by the need to find or supply some information to a pilot or someone else he or she is working with. Many times I have made a transmission and received no acknowledgment from the controller. When that happens I bug the controller until I get the acknowledgment I am seeking. A controller not responding to a pilot's transmission is just as bad for safe communications as the reverse. Perhaps the controller was not listening to the response of the pilot who was charged with the altitude violation. He may have been distracted at the moment the response was given and assumed it was the proper one. If that was the case then my friend should never have been charged with the violation because the controller did not verify that the instruction he gave was received correctly.

Acknowledging a transmission is like reading back a clearance. Both parties must understand that the information was received properly. This is particularly true of amended clearances, and altitude and frequency changes. If there is a breakdown in the readback process, conflicts arise, such as altitude deviation. Be certain that you listen for and acknowledge any instructions you are given by ATC, and if you have any question about the validity of the information be certain to clarify it.

Aircraft don't have to be airborne for poor communications to interfere with safe operation. In the last several years there have been several major accidents resulting from aircraft occupying space on a runway while another aircraft was landing on it. Some of those accidents occurred when pilots misunderstood a communication, while others were the result of controllers instructing an aircraft to taxi into position on the runway and then forgetting it was there. Don't think you are safe because you are still on the ground. Be just as vigilant about monitoring communications anywhere on the airport. And if you are told to taxi into position and hold, listen carefully to the tower frequency for evidence of another airplane being cleared to land on your runway. Don't let too much time go by after that occurs before you ask the controller about your clearance to take off. I can tell you why from personal experience.

In the late 1970s I was flying a Cessna 421 for an east coast corporation. I flew a trip into Detroit Metro Airport to drop off some passengers, to be followed by a deadhead leg home. The trip into Metro was uneventful. I got my outbound clearance on the clearance delivery frequency and taxied out according to my instructions. At the runway I did my runup and called the tower to tell the controller I was ready to take off. "50 Juliet, taxi into position and hold on 3 Right," came the response.

The controller cleared a flight to land on the runway where I was positioned and holding.

Before that day I never thought about a position-and-hold clearance. I taxied into position and waited. It is not unusual at a major airport to sit in position for a minute or two, especially if more than one runway is in use for takeoffs. After a minute and a half or so the controller cleared a Northwest flight to land on 3 Right, but still he did not clear me for takeoff. I started getting nervous because I had no idea how far out the airliner was. After another 30 seconds went by I called the tower and said, "How about the takeoff clearance for 50 Juliet on 3 Right?" The controller replied in an urgent voice, "50 Juliet, cleared for immediate takeoff." He had forgotten all about me. The lesson was to listen up as carefully on the ground as you do in the air.

Don't fail to communicate with ground control if you suddenly realize that you don't know where you are on the airport. This usually occurs when the visibility is poor and the controller cannot see you. If you have any question about your position on the airport check to be certain you are not on a runway, then stop and call the controller for help. Don't cross a runway unless you know for certain that you have been cleared to cross it. Whenever in doubt in the air or on the ground, communicate with ATC.

Some pilots have stereo setups that allow them to listen to music, broadcast radio, or whatever while they are flying along. DON'T do this when flying IFR. Outside entertainment sources can interfere with your reception of a clearance. And what if the controller needed to reach you quickly to advise you to take evasive action from conflicting traffic? You might not get the message.

In an earlier chapter we discussed professionalism. Communicating with ATC requires that from each of us who uses the system. And if something occurs that you want to discuss with the ATC controller, don't do it on the air. Ask for a phone number and call him or her after you get on the ground. Discussing a problem over an open radio channel prevents the use of that frequency by others and may prevent the orderly flow of traffic and interfere with safety of flight. If a controller is very busy or denies your request, if you want to argue with him or her do it on the telephone after the flight is completed. Don't risk your safety, that of your passengers, and possibly other airplanes working the same ATC sector by tying up the frequency with a prolonged argument. At the same time if something is occurring that will have an immediate and definite impact on the safety of flight, don't hesitate to take whatever action is necessary if you are unable to get the controller's attention or if he or she refuses to help you. You can always sort that out on the ground over the telephone after the airplane is safely on the ground.

In the air lives can depend on clear, concise communication. Be sure you understand the procedures and techniques that apply to working within the ATC system. Never accept a clearance that you cannot comply with, and ask for clarification whenever you are given instructions that do not make sense to you. Keep your transmissions short and to the point, and always be aware of what is going on around you by listening to the transmissions of others on the same frequency you are working. Make good communications a high priority in your instrument flying.

CHAPTER ELEVEN

INSTRUMENT TAKEOFFS

The busiest time in the cockpit is during landing and takeoff. Some pilots would tell you that during an instrument approach is when the pilot works the hardest. That may be true given the length of time involved in the approach, but I think that during the shorter period of the takeoff and initial climb the workload is actually heavier than on the approach, especially when you consider very low ceilings and visibilities.

Pilots who operate under Federal Aviation Regulations (FARs) Part 91, those who don't fly for hire, are allowed to take off with no visibility. The workload during a zero/zero takeoff is probably the highest a pilot will experience, especially if he or she is operating without the assistance of a second pilot. The time and place for a zero/zero takeoff must be carefully chosen, and the pilot who decides to take off with the weather that low must be current and very proficient in the airplane he or she is flying. There probably are few non-professional pilots who have such an urgent need to depart when there is no ceiling or visibility. Most IFR departures in IMC are considered low-visibility takeoffs.

Is there such a thing as a normal takeoff in IFR conditions? To professional pilots, those who fly day after day for a living, any instrument takeoff might be routine, while to others the word "normal" may not apply to any takeoffs made in IFR conditions.

Although a single-pilot zero/zero takeoff is legal, I highly recommend that you don't attempt it.

A zero/zero takeoff certainly would not be considered normal, mainly because it is not a routine operation. Although it is legal for a single pilot to make a zero/zero takeoff, I highly recommend that you don't attempt it. Because so many things can go so wrong so fast during a zero/zero takeoff, I would not attempt it unless I was flying a two-pilot airplane equipped with redundant flight instruments for both pilots to reference, and there was a very compelling reason for the departure under those conditions. The second pilot is necessary to monitor the performance of the aircraft while the first pilot does the flying. The non-flying pilot should call out significant airspeeds, check the engine instruments to ensure that all indications are normal, and monitor the aircraft's direction on the runway.

In addition to the actual work of getting the airplane off the ground in zero/zero conditions, the next problem is: where do you go if you have a mechanical problem right after takeoff? It is imperative that you have a takeoff alternate close to the departure point. It is usually hard to find one because fog normally overspreads wide areas, except some localized conditions that may be due to water or terrain in the vicinity of the airport.

In my 26 years of flying I don't think I have done more than three zero/zero takeoffs. All of them were in turbine powered airplanes that were capable of climbing away from the earth's surface rapidly. One of them featured an obscured ceiling with zero visibility, and as we climbed through 50 feet or so we were in the clear.

How quickly you can climb affects how successful any low visibility instrument takeoff will be. A heavily loaded piston engine airplane that will not climb well in that state is not a good candidate. If the airplane falters even slightly coming out of ground effect, it might settle back to the ground. But whatever airplane you fly, go right to the best angle-of-climb speed and keep it there until you are sure the aircraft is at a safe altitude and that all obstacles have been cleared.

Now, back to the question of what is a normal takeoff under instrument conditions. In the final analysis it will depend on the pilot's experience level, the airplane flown, currency and proficiency, and what the pilot's personal limits demand before a takeoff can begin. There probably is no such thing as a normal takeoff that fits all instrument pilots. For example, an airline pilot who flies daily is likely to take off when the conditions meet legal and company requirements as they are designated in the company operations manual. But a non-professional pilot who does not fly IFR regularly will need to analyze each situation, and the accompanying weather, to determine if a safe takeoff can be made.

There are so many weather variables to be be evaluated that every takeoff is different, even if the apparent ceiling and visibility are the same. The wind would play a major factor in any decision to take off on the gages, especially if there is high terrain on the downwind side of the runway. Runway conditions, NOTAMS for the airport and surrounding area, velocity of falling rain or snow, and any severe weather in the area all must be considered. So, is there such a thing as a normal takeoff in instrument conditions? Probably not.

I alluded to the workload during a zero/zero takeoff before. It is very intense for a relatively short period, and the only difference between a zero/zero takeoff and any other instrument takeoff is your ability to monitor your progress on the runway by looking outside the windscreen instead of at the instruments. Often when the visibility is reduced you will break ground and instantly lose sight of the runway, requiring an immediate transition to the instruments. So, there is not a great deal of difference in workload between a zero/zero takeoff and a low visibility takeoff.

Many pilots use landing minimums
as their takeoff requirement.

By the way, for this discussion I consider a low visibility takeoff to be one made when conditions are at landing minimums for the runway being used. For example, if the runway has an ILS approach with an 1,800 RVR requirement for landing, a low visibility takeoff would be a launch at landing minimums. That is a good number to focus on because many pilots use landing minimums as their takeoff requirement. If they take off and have some kind of problem that demands an immediate landing, they should be able to return to the same runway using the designated approach.

So, what is the difference between a low visibility takeoff and a zero/zero takeoff? It is the method of keeping the airplane aligned with the runway until liftoff. Sometimes the fog can be so thick that the runway is not visible, while at other times, usually during daylight hours, you will see the runway centerline stripe and nothing more. A low visibility takeoff usually affords a continuous view of the runway until rotation.

But think about this. If you have no reference to the runway during the takeoff roll and your directional gyro is not working exactly right, what is to keep you from running off the side of the runway? That is why the second pair of eyes and instruments is necessary.

So, we are back to workload again. The pilot making a zero/zero takeoff has a higher workload only because he or she cannot see the runway well. If the centerline stripe is visible that makes it easier, and I would not consider a zero/zero takeoff on a runway where the centerline stripe is not clear.

After liftoff the workload remains high until the airplane is clear of all obstacles, has reached a safe climb speed, and can be configured for normal climb. Only then can the pilot relax to the point where routine IFR operations can begin. The workload for the pilot making a low visibility takeoff is the same from rotation to the point where normal IFR operations begin.

Some instrument takeoffs are easier than others. For example, if the ceiling is 1,000 feet and the visibility below it is 3 miles or better, you are likely to have the airplane configured for climb before you enter the clouds. The workload on that takeoff is much lighter than it would be on the low visibility or zero/zero takeoff, because from the time you release your brakes until the airplane is configured for climb as you enter the clouds you are in visual conditions.

But there are times when the ceiling may be 1,000 feet but the visibility is reduced in fog or some form of precipitation. As you begin the takeoff roll there may be plenty of visual cues on the surface, but as soon as you break ground that will all change. Whether you realize it or not you are back to the low visibility takeoff. Your personal limits must deal with those conditions, especially if you don't feel comfortable going on the gages immediately after the wheels leave the ground.

I am not telling you about low visibility and zero/zero takeoffs so you will rush right out and do them. In fact, my purpose is just the opposite. I want you to know how difficult they are and understand that before you attempt to do one you should be absolutely certain that you need to take off in those conditions, and that there are no doubts in your mind about being able to accomplish it safely. If you are not up to par anything unusual that occurs on or near the ground is likely to cause a fatal accident.

Do you know exactly where the trim settings should be for your airplane's load?

Now let's look at some associated factors that must be considered when making any instrument takeoff. First is weight and balance. Are you thoroughly familiar with how your airplane feels with the load you are going to put in it? Do you know exactly where the trim settings should be for that load? The elevator trim setting and the aircraft loading will have a great influence on the pitch attitude that is attained during rotation and liftoff. If you are making a zero/zero or low visibility takeoff it will be very difficult for you to correct any deficiency during or right after takeoff. You will be very busy without having to deal with an out-of-trim condition. If the weather features higher ceilings and visibilities it will not be as much of a problem, because your workload will be a little lighter if you can maintain visual contact with the ground until after a normal climb is established.

It is very important that the loading be within the aircraft's limits. Remember, the farther aft the center of gravity (CG) is the harder it will be to control the aircraft. There have been accidents caused by excessive aft loadings during instrument takeoffs. In many aircraft it is difficult to get an excessive forward CG, but it may be possible in yours. Be certain that you are within your aircraft's weight and balance limits before takeoff. And don't just add up the weights of your passengers, fuel, and baggage to determine if you are under gross weight. Do the entire calculation to be certain the aircraft is within CG limits.

If you overrotate and the aircraft pitches up more than you intend, the airplane will be slow to accelerate, and it may stall if the attitude is too high. If you allow this to happen during a zero/zero or low visibility takeoff it might not be apparent to you right away, and the delay in reacting to the condition could result in an accident.

The reason for that is your workload. While you need to be scanning your instruments there are other things going on as well. You are watching the engine gages to make sure power is normal, you may be transitioning from outside to inside, and it takes time to establish a scan. Problems usually occur the instant the pilot realizes that the nose is too high. He or she instinctively over-reacts and pushes the nose down too much and too quickly. Then the airplane starts a descent, and at worst contacts the runway again or some terrain along the departure path. But usually it does a wheelbarrow-type maneuver while the pilot tries to find the right attitude and maintain it. Low timers or pilots who are not proficient enough for the weather they are flying in fall victim to that phenomenon.

If the pilot does not rotate the nose enough the aircraft will remain on the ground much longer than it should. That also occurs when the trim is set too far forward. Then, the pilot pulls on the yoke to the point where the airplane jumps off the ground unexpectedly. Some pilots panic at that point because they are afraid of getting the nose too high and do the same as the pilot who has the trim set too far back. They push forward on the yoke, and the airplane contacts the runway again.

So, the key to any instrument takeoff is familiarity with the airplane you are flying. The problems I have just described normally don't happen to those who know their airplanes thoroughly and perform their checklists meticulously before takeoff.

Check your systems before departing. You don't want any surprises when airborne.

Before departing into IFR conditions you must check to make sure that all the flight instruments, avionics, and other systems are working properly. You don't want any surprises when you get airborne and need to rely on a piece of equipment that is not serviceable. For example, if you have electric flight instruments the first step is to make sure that the alternator is functioning properly. To do this you simply load it by turning on a couple of high-draw systems such as the landing lights and pitot heat. You want to see the alternator increase its output to meet the load. That should be apparent on the ammeter. Then check each instrument, once it has had time to spool up, for proper indication. If you lose your alternator in flight it will not be long before those instruments and the other radio equipment draw the battery down to the point where nothing will work. If the attitude indicator is not working properly before a low visibility takeoff you could fly the airplane into the ground by trying to follow its indications.

Suction instruments must be checked as well. Most light airplanes sport vacuum or pressure-driven flight instruments. If the vacuum or air source fails typically you will lose the attitude and direction indicators. Fortunately there is a standby vaccum source available for most aircraft that directs suction from the engine's manifold to the instruments in the event of a vacuum pump failure. I had one of those installed in my Piper Arrow and am happy with the way it operates. I highly recommend a standby vacuum source to any aircraft owner who flies IFR in a single engine airplane. It could save you the hassle of having to fly partial panel if your vacuum pump quits while you are in the clouds.

In many locations it is difficult to check avionics for proper operation before each takeoff because there are no facilities on the field. So, it is important that you monitor their operation during flight and correct any defects after landing so you know that all the equipment is operating properly for the next flight.

Directional control on the runway can be a major problem for a pilot who is attempting to take off in low visibility conditions. In VFR conditions your forward and peripheral vision give you immediate input if the airplane leaves the centerline of the runway. In very low visibility conditions, especially if there is no centerline stripe, it is very difficult to tell if you are not maintaining alignment on the runway. Increasing power in a light single and not adding enough right rudder will allow the aircraft to drift to the left. The amount of drift will depend on the amount of rudder that is applied.

In twins, if both engines don't accelerate at the

same rate the airplane can drift one way or the other depending on which engine is supplying less power. That happens when there are splits in the throttles. If there is more than a quarter inch of difference between the two throttles at a given engine setting, chances are the power will be uneven. If you plan on doing any low visibility takeoffs in your twin make sure you have your mechanic "equalize" the engines so that as you push the throttles forward the power output from each engine is the same.

One way of getting the takeoff roll underway with good runway alignment is to hold the brakes, bring the power up to some pre-determined level, then release the brakes. With most types that will give you immediate rudder authority when the airplane starts to move, making it easier to maintain the centerline stripe.

What you do has to depend on how much runway you have left.

What happens if you notice a system failure during the takeoff roll? You will have to make a snap decision to either continue the takeoff or abort, depending on the circumstances. If you are flying a piston engine airplane and lose engine power there is little doubt about what you will do no matter where in the takeoff roll you are, as long as the wheels are still on the ground. But what if a door pops open? What you do has to depend on how much runway you have left.

In the case of the open door, if you don't have room to stop safely most airplanes will fly with little or no noticeable difference. You can make the takeoff, return to land, shut the door, and depart again.

That is, if you have landing minimums. If you don't it might be a long ride with a lot of noise and cold air in the cabin. That is another reason to use a checklist before takeoff.

The point is that you must make an on-the spot-decision when something occurs during takeoff and hope that it is the right one. Often pilots have rejected a takeoff and run off the runway, causing injuries and damage to the aircraft, after some problem developed. In retrospect, FAA and NTSB investigators look at the aircraft performance charts and whatever occurred that required an abort, then decide what the pilot should or should not have done. It is a little late for that. As a pilot you must make the decision on the spot and live with it. The more familiar you are with the airplane you are flying the more knowledge you will have to use in dealing with that situation.

I remember two incidents that might give you more insight into aborting during takeoff. The first occurred in Elmira, New York years ago. I was flying a Cessna 421. It was a cold and dreary winter day with VFR conditions and occasional light snow showers. Everything checked out normally during the runup and I called for takeoff clearance. As I pushed the throttles up and started rolling on the runway the nose of the airplane started yawing to the right. I counteracted it with rudder, but the more power I called for the worse the yaw became. I looked at the engine gages and saw that the right engine was not making power, so I pulled both throttles to idle, aborted the takeoff, and taxied in to the ramp.

A mechanic pulled the cowl down on the right engine and found a broken exhaust pipe, a common problem with that model of airplane in the mid-1970s. My passengers ended up going out on a commercial flight while I stayed overnight and waited for the replacement part.

The runway was long enough and the problem showed up early in the takeoff roll, so there was no question of being able to stop on the pavement. In fact, if you fly an airplane with a turbo-charged engine and experience a major loss of manifold pressure while increasing power during the takeoff roll, your best option is likely to be aborting the takeoff. While the problem could be a turbo-charger or waste gate malfunction, if it is a broken exhaust system and you continue the takeoff you probably will wind up with a fire under the cowling. If you become airborne with a fire burning in the engine compartment you might not have enough time to get around the traffic pattern to make a safe landing.

On another day I was ferrying the same airplane 12 miles from North Central State Airport to Providence, Rhode Island for a passenger pickup. The runway in use was 15, a 3,200-foot paved strip. The winds were strong out of the southeast and it had been raining heavily.

I had my instrument clearance and taxied out onto the wet runway. I selected takeoff power and started rolling. Just as I rotated I heard several thuds, but the airplane continued to operate normally so I took off and flew to Providence. When I got there I inspected the airplane and found a minor ding in the leading edge of the left wing. I called back to North Central's operations office and the airport manager told me that the runway crew retrieved five sea gulls from the left side of the runway. I was fortunate that there was not more damage to the aircraft, but more important, had I aborted the takeoff at the point where the birds hit the airplane, I would have run off the end of the runway and caused more damage than the collision with the birds. The more familiar you are with your airplane and how it operates, the faster and safer will be the judgments you make when the unexpected occurs.

Always fly the airplane first,
no matter what else is happening.

During any phase of flight it is vital that you always fly the airplane first, no matter what else is happening. While taking off you are so close to the ground that any distraction that occurs can have a devastating effect on the outcome of the flight. If you allow your attention to be drawn away from physically manipulating the aircraft's controls you will be in serious trouble. Even the failure of an engine in a twin near the ground requires that you continue to fly the airplane first. Yes, you must act quickly to clean up the airplane, but if you don't continue to fly it while you are doing the emergency drill it may stall or roll over if the speed gets below VMC.

Emergency situations that occur during the takeoff usually are the result of poor cockpit and checklist procedures. Most of them can be avoided by careful attention to detail before the pilot commits to the takeoff roll. You certainly don't want to have any problems near the ground during an instrument takeoff where the ceiling and visibility are low, so get in the habit of using a good checklist before takeoff.

Instrument takeoffs are different from those you do in VFR conditions. You must have a higher awareness level, be capable of flying the airplane on instruments as soon as it lifts off the runway during low visibility conditions, clean the airplane up and deal with normal after-takeoff duties such as establishing communications with ATC, while watching for anything that indicates a problem is developing in one of the airplane's systems. The workload is much higher than what you experience during a VFR takeoff, because so much of your attention must be devoted to the instrument panel instead of outside the windshield. So be certain you are up to the task when you decide to make a low visibility takeoff, and leave the zero/zero departures for more experienced pilots.

CHAPTER TWELVE

INSTRUMENT LANDINGS

Instrument approaches are our link back to the earth's surface. We can depart an airport in low IFR con ditions and fly in the clouds until we are near or over our destination, but then we must get down safely without striking the ground or another object. Most accidents occur during the takeoff or landing phase of flight because the airplane is so close to the surface that any miscalculation by the pilot can result in unintended contact with the terrain or a manmade object that happens to be in the flight path.

Too many pilots have tried descending through clouds without clearances in an attempt to find some recognizable landmarks that would lead them to the airport they sought.

Pilots may have various reasons for choosing that illegal, dangerous, and often fatal path back to the earth's surface that can result in what we call controlled flight into terrain. But when a rescue team has to be sent out to recover the aircraft, crew, and passengers, whatever motivation was behind the pilot's decision to descend into the clouds and "feel" for the earth's surface makes little difference.

Instrument approaches remove the fear of striking terrain that we did or did not know was there and the need to illegally descend through clouds in search of visual landmarks to point us towards an airport. Most of the approaches we fly have the same basic elements. They all offer a method of transitioning from the enroute phase of flight to the approach. In some situations the pilot is responsible for the transformation, but much of the time he or she will be radar vectored to the final approach course. The controller's direction provides terrain clearance as well as separation from other aircraft. In either case the pilot must have good situational and positional awareness, to be certain that the procedure is followed to the letter and that the controller is not misguiding the flight.

The approach phase normally offers some method of course reversal so aircraft coming from a direction that is different from the final approach course can become properly aligned with the runway or airport. In a radar environment the controller will vector the aircraft to the final approach course, but there are still places and times where radar services are not available, so pilots must understand the method of course reversal in use for a particular approach and be capable of successfully completing it.

The final approach phase is designed to position the airplane within the boundaries of the airport or in alignment with a particular runway. The type of approach in use, and surrounding terrain or other features, determine how low the airplane may descend in its quest for the airport.

Many factors determine what type of approach procedure a pilot uses at a given airport. The type of equipment installed in the aircraft is probably the primary consideration, followed by the availability of approaches at the destination, and both will be directly affected by the weather and winds in the area of the landing site.

The ILS approach still offers the pilot the most precision.

Instrument approaches have not changed a great deal over the years, though there are many more airports today that may be accessed in inclement weather than there were 30 years ago. The ILS approach still offers the pilot the most precision because when it is flown properly the airplane will descend along a predetermined corridor to as low as 200 feet above the surface.

And then there is the missed approach. Too often pilots pay little attention to this procedure until it is time to do it. Why? Because most approaches are successful, and if the weather at the destination is known to be good, pilots decide too early that they will land there and that the missed approach procedure will not be necessary.

Transitioning from the enroute portion of a flight to the approach portion can be tricky in many places, especially where mountainous terrain exists. It is in places like these where our modern radar systems lack the ability to see through the terrain. Once an airplane descends below the radar coverage for the area, the pilot becomes responsible for maintaining the required clearance from the surface below. In flat terrain, where the airport is far removed from the radar site, the controller may only see the airplane if it is above a certain altitude because of transmission and reception limits of the system he or she is using. While the terrain threats are not as severe as in the mountains, if the pilot is not adept at operating without radar coverage he or she could run into trouble before getting safely to the airport.

The procedure turn and holding pattern are the two most popular types of course reversal used in non-radar environments. Many procedure turns have been removed from approach plates and replaced with holding patterns. That is because the holding pattern reversal requires less maneuvering space than does the procedure turn, though the pilot's workload is higher.

Some approaches don't offer course reversals. That means the pilot must fly to the initial approach fix to begin the approach, and that could be several miles or more out of the way depending on the approach and airport layout.

A procedure turn is the simpler of the course reversals (see Figure 1). The pilot flies outbound on the final approach course for a time he or she determines based on the wind direction and speed. Then a 45-degree turn is made followed by a 180-degree turn.

Then the final approach course is intercepted and flown inbound to complete the approach.

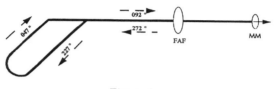

Figure 1
Procedure Turn Course Reversal

The holding pattern course reversal (see Figure 2) is more complicated because of the entry procedure used. What entry procedure you use depends on the direction you are approaching the holding pattern fix from. There'll be more on holding pattern entries in Chapter Twenty.

Figure 2
Holding Pattern Course Reversal

Many approaches offer pilots terminal routings that lead to instrument approaches where no procedure turn is required. The letters NoPT are the designator. When no procedure turn is required you cannot do one without approval from ATC.

Terminal radar saves pilots much time in the air because it allows controllers to vector airplanes one after the other to the final approach course. But pilots often become too dependent on radar and allow complacency to rob them of situational and positional awareness.

For example, the center controller hands you off to the local approach controller while you are still about 40 miles from your landing airport. If you don't keep track of where you are in relation to the airport and the approach you are going to fly, how do you know when to slow down or configure the airplane for landing? Those are two critical elements in any approach, because if you configure for landing too soon your reduced airspeed may delay others behind you. Or, you might be pulled out of the sequence and placed behind faster traffic. If you wait too long to put the gear and flaps down your airspeed on final approach will be too high, you will have a tough time flying the approach, and you might be forced to go around because of poor approach alignment. If the runway is short and you do locate it you might run off the end because you could not get the airplane stopped on it.

Positional awareness is even more important in a non-radar environment.

Positional awareness is even more important when you are operating in a non-radar environment. If you don't know exactly where you are when the controller speaks the words "radar services terminated" then I doubt you can complete the instrument approach successfully.

Some pilots who always operate in a radar environment have problems when they suddenly find themselves without a controller's guidance. That became painfully obvious in 1974 when a Boeing 727 struck high terrain while descending into Dulles Airport. The airplane had been cleared for the VOR/DME approach to Runway 12 when the crew descended below the minimum safe altitude for the area they were flying in. Because they were cleared for the approach the captain thought they could descend to 1,800 feet, that which is designated as the final approach fix crossing altitude on the approach plate. They should have been at 3,400 feet at the point where they struck the terrain. There will be more on non-radar operations in Chapter Seventeen.

While vectoring you for an approach the controller may clear you to descend to altitudes below those shown as safe or appropriate on your approach plate. Often controllers have what are called minimum vectoring altitudes that are used at their convenience for separation or as an aid to a pilot who is about to fly a visual approach into an airport. For example, if you are cleared to 3,000 feet and you are still in the clouds or see hints of the ground showing through occaisional bases, if the controller has a lower minimum vectoring altitude, say 2,700 feet, you probably can get below the clouds, find the airport, and accept the visual approach instead of taking the time to go out for a complete approach.

I flew a Cessna 421 into Alamogordo, New Mexico a few years ago. I was at 10,000 feet flying west toward the mountains that ring the area around the airport when I noticed on my chart that the MEA for that area was 12,000 feet. Since the controller did not ask me to climb to 12,000 feet I asked him if 10,000 feet was an acceptable altitude in lieu of the MEA. He said it was. I was in the clouds and could not see the terrain. Once I passed the ridge line, he cleared me for the VOR Runway 3 approach into Alamogordo. The mountains were obscured by cloud, and I did not see how high they were until the next morning when the weather cleared. That was certainly not a place you want to make a mistake regarding safe altitudes. So, any time you see a discrepancy between your chart or approach plate and an altitude that a controller has cleared you to, make sure you ask him or her about it. Like always knowing where you are in relation to the airport or final fix, it is just as important to know that the altitudes issued by the controller are proper.

Without the approach plate you cannot do an approach. A friend of mine told me the tale of a fellow he flew with in a Cessna 310 who did not have approach plates for Minneapolis. He filed there anyway. When approach control was vectoring him for an ILS to Runway 29 Left he called the controller and told him that he spilled coffee on his plate and obliterated the ILS frequency. The controller provided that, and the pilot flew the approach with no information whatsoever about decision height, final fix crossing altitude, or the missed approach procedure. A very dangerous thing to do. My friend said the ceiling at Minneapolis that day was about 700 feet.

Another pilot, when questioned by his first-time co-pilot as to where the approach plates were for the airport they were approaching in Indiana, replied that they weren't necessary. "We're in a jet," the Citation Captain said. "We'll be vectored right to the runway."

The first thing I do as I begin the preflight inspection is make sure I have the plates and charts that I

will need for the entire flight. Since I fly many different airplanes I usually carry my own, but occasionally
my charts don't cover an area I am flying to. Either I
have to buy the coverage I need or use what is in the
airplane. Usually I buy what I need ahead of time so I
don't get to the airplane on the day of the trip and find
that the pilot took his home to update them, or that
those on board are not current.

*Shortly after configuring the airplane
for cruise, I pull out the plates for the
destination airport.*

Shortly after configuring the airplane for cruising flight, no matter how short or long the flight is, I
put away the plates for my departure airport and pull
out the ones for the destination airport. I look over the
approaches that are available and the general layout of
the airport, though I probably have already done that
as part of my flight planning. I take out all the approach plates because I don't know which one I will be
using at that point. If I get into the terminal area, find
that there has been a switch because of a wind or
weather change, I don't have to dig back into the book
for the correct one when I need to be flying the airplane.
        I get the ATIS as far out as possible so I can
find out what the weather is doing and which approach
is in use. Then I review the approach that I expect to
fly. The first thing I look at is the minimum sector
altitude(s) (MSAs) (see Figure 3) that tell me what the
lowest safe altitudes are within a 25 nautical mile radius of a depicted navigational fix. The MSA also guar-

antees me a 1,000-foot obstacle clearance within that radius. Then I look over the approach itself for anything that might be unusual, such as obstacles or terrain that could affect how the approach is flown, or notes that may alter the approach procedure depending on information that is or is not available, such as a local altimeter setting. I take a quick look at the procedure itself, the approach course headings, and minimums.

Figure 3
Minimum Sector Altitudes

When I am handed off to the approach facility that will see me through the transition from the enroute phase of the flight to the approach phase, I review the approach plate. I start with the approach frequency, which I dial into the nav radio I will use. Then I study all aspects of the procedure including the outbound and inbound headings, fixes I may need to use, and whatever altitudes I may need to be aware of, such as crossing altitudes at the initial approach or final fixes, and decision height or minimum descent altitude. Also, I look for special equipment requirements such as notes stating that an ADF, distance measuring equipment (DME), or another piece of equipment is required.

*Accidents have happened because
pilots set their nav radios to a local
VOR instead of the ILS frequency.*

When the controller starts vectoring me for the
approach I set up whatever radios or equipment I will
need during the approach. I double check all frequencies and OBS settings to make sure they are correct.
Accidents have occurred because pilots set their nav
radios to a local VOR instead of to the proper ILS frequency.

In most of the airplanes I fly there is a clip to
hold the approach plate to the control yoke so I can
review the plate whenever I wish without having to look
too far away from the instrument panel. The plate
should be kept within viewing range. Having the book
of plates open and sitting on the right seat is too distracting when I need to refer to the procedure.

Positional awareness becomes critical at this
point because it is where I have to start thinking about
slowing the airplane and reconfiguring it for landing.
Exactly where I begin the checklist depends on the type
of airplane I am flying. I don't want to wait until I am
established on the final approach course to begin the
transition from enroute to approach. If I don't keep
track of my position while being vectored I will not
know where I am until I intercept the final approach
course.

If I am flying a Baron, Mooney, or any airplane
that is difficult to slow down, I try to get down to the
altitude I will cross the final fix at earlier than I normally would. That is because it takes a while to reduce the airspeed, and I don't like to pull the power

back in large increments or the engine(s) cool too fast. So I plan as far ahead as possible for the traffic situation and the weather. Remember that each type of aircraft demands different strategies, and that is why it is so important to know the airplane you are flying thoroughly.

At some high density airports ATC may ask you to keep your speed up to facilitate high-speed traffic behind you. It is up to the controller to be certain there is enough space between arriving aircraft, but most pilots try to accommodate the request whenever possible. If a controller asks me to maintain a certain speed to the outer marker or final approach fix that is above my initial flap operating or gear extension speed, whichever is higher, I refuse. Instead I offer to fly at or below my initial flap operating speed. That is usually acceptable to the controller and allows me to quickly reduce to final approach speed at the fix.

If you are flying a fixed gear airplane you can slow it quickly by applying flaps and reducing power, but watch how quickly you pull the power back on a piston engine, especially in winter. With a retractable it's a little tougher because some of them don't like to slow down. Don't allow the controller to bully you into flying a speed to the final approach fix that is not going to allow you enough time or space to slow the airplane before you begin the final descent.

An ILS approach demands much of the pilot's attention from the time he or she tunes in the radios until the airplane is taxied off the runway. For the uninitiated, or those who don't practice too often, it is a difficult approach to do properly. The secret behind a good ILS approach is knowing what descent rate you need to maintain to remain on the glide slope, and what heading you need to fly to keep the localizer needle centered. If you know those, there is no reason why you should not be capable of flying a decent approach, provided you are competent at flying your airplane on the gages.

Any instrument approach is a challenge because the conditions are never the same, even if you fly the same one repeatedly. The ILS is particularly challenging because of the narrow beam width that is radiated. The closer the airplane gets to the system's antenna the more sensitive the needles get. That means that the pilot must have the heading and descent rate figured out before getting too far along the approach, or he or she will be chasing the needle.

Chasing the needle on an ILS is not a good practice.

Chasing the needle on an ILS is not a good practice because it robs your attention from other duties, for one thing, and can lead to a descent into the terrain below if you let the airplane get too far below the glide slope.

If your directional gyro is set correctly, and you should check it before beginning any approach, it should not take but a few seconds to figure out what heading you need to fly to stay on the localizer. I do it with slight heading changes, using just a little rudder pressure to change the heading one or two degrees in the direction the localizer needle is going. If you have a very strong crosswind you might need more correction, but most of the time you don't need much.

If you would like a pictorial demonstration of how much correction is needed on a localizer approach, fly one in VFR conditions without your view limiting device. Look at the runway ahead as you correct for the wind. You will see just how little crab it takes to maintain the localizer. Then fly one with the hood on. Remember to keep your corrections small. Most pilots make changes in minimum increments of five or even 10 degrees. Often that is too much and they wind up flying back through the localizer, with the help of the wind, but they don't realize it right away because they are looking at their other instruments or the approach plate. When they see the needle has swung the other way they turn back 20 degrees and fly through the course again, albeit a little slower because now they are flying more into the wind. But all the way down the approach they are going back and forth because they don't understand the airplane's true relationship to the runway, and that the pictorial in front of them on the instruments is presented at a different resolution than when they can see the runway and the horizon visually.

The easiest way to find the right heading for the approach you are flying is to start with the inbound course heading. Let's call that the true heading. If you have been paying attention during the flight you will have some idea of where the wind is. Knowing this you can even put a couple of degrees of correction in as you turn to the heading. Call the result your magnetic heading. Then see which way the needle goes. If it stays centered initially you have done a good job "scoping" out the winds. If it moves to one side or the other the rate of movement should determine how much correction you make. If it moves rapidly you have a good crosswind and you will want to turn toward the needle until it stops its movement. But seldom is the total difference between the true heading and magnetic heading more than 10 degrees. I have seen approaches where more was required, but that is very unusual.

Once the needle movement stops, turn toward the needle another one or two degrees to get it to start back toward the center. Then, as the needle approaches the on-course position, remove half of the difference between your magnetic heading and the true heading. Don't round it off by using increments of five to stay on an easy heading to fly. If you want to be on the center of the localizer you must fly the exact heading it takes. Remember to make very small adjustments with a tap on the rudder pedal in the direction you want to go. If you bank the airplane for a one- or two-degree correction you will likely overfly the heading you want and start chasing the needle.

The wind is likely to change as you start your descent on the glide slope. Most of the time you can anticipate which way it will go by comparing the known wind direction aloft, which you estimate by considering the differential between the true heading and the magnetic heading that keeps you aligned on the localizer, and the wind direction reported on the surface. If they are approximately the same there is likely to be little change on the approach. If they are different be prepared for the shift.

That is not a hard and fast rule, though. There could be a couple of wind shears between the surface and your final approach fix crossing altitude. If you don't recognize that, you can become confused and wind up with a full-needle deflection before you know it. A full-needle deflection means an automatic go-around.

I fly the glide slope much the same way as the localizer. But instead of a heading for a reference point I use a rate of descent based on the angle of the glide slope adjusted for the airspeed I will be flying. For example, the ILS to Runway 9 Right at Pontiac, Michigan offers a three-degree glide slope. At 100 knots on the final approach course a descent rate of approximately 550 feet per minute will keep me on the glide slope. That is with no wind. So, I start with that, make a correction for the wind and go from there. I make my attitude changes very small when trying to keep the needle in the center, and change my rate of descent by no more than 50 feet per minute up or down at any one time if the needle moves off the center.

On most ILS approaches I can start with a 500- to 600-feet per minute rate of descent.

NOS approach plates (see Figure 4) don't offer rate of descent information on the individual chart (the information is at the back of the book) while Jeppesen plates do, but on most ILS approaches I can start with a 500- to 600-feet per minute rate of descent, and I know it will be pretty close. I always fly the glide slope using a desired rate of descent, subtracting from it or adding to it as the needle indication changes. Just watching the needle change without having a reference rate of descent results in overcontrolling and chasing the glide slope needle. Except in unusual wind conditions I never allow the rate of descent to increase or

decrease more than 100 feet per minute from the reference. That will ensure that I don't try to climb too
steeply into the glide slope or dive at it. If I do either
I will probably go through it and wind up with a full-
needle deflection.

How quickly you can scan your instruments will
determine how well you do an ILS approach. Most
pilots have problems because while they are looking at
something else, one or both needles start to move off
their centered positions. When they again look at the
OBS they see what has happened, panic because they
are off course, then overcorrect in an attempt to get
back on course quickly. That is when the needle chasing begins. In fact, often the pilot fixates on the ILS at
that point and forgets to scan the rest of the instruments. That results in poor heading, attitude, and altitude control.

The more practice ILS approaches you do the
better you will feel when you are faced with doing the
real thing. Currency and proficiency are extremely
important with this type of approach if you expect to
do it well. You cannot become proficient while you
are trying to do an ILS for real unless it is in a training
situation. The anxiety factors are too high. The only
time you know where you are on the approach is when
the needles are centered. If you get too far below the
glide slope you could hit the terrain, and if you get too
far above it you will not see the runway.

Non-precision approaches are not quite as difficult because the descent is from one specified altitude
to another with no vertical guidance. Except for the
localizer approach the course widths are usually broader
with a less sensitive needle. That means the needle

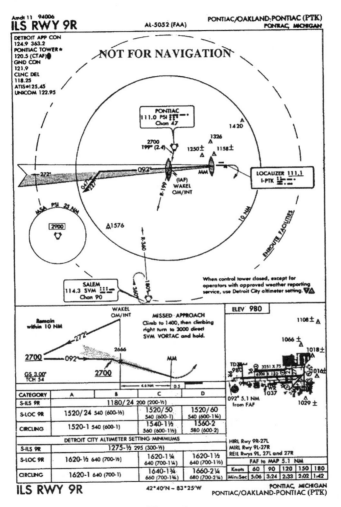

Figure 4
Rate Of Descent Information Is Not Given on NOS Plates
But Time From Final Approach Fix To The Missed Approach
Point Is Listed

does not show a course differential as rapidly as the localizer needle, although one still may be there.

The horizontal portion of the non-precision approach is flown the same way as the localizer with a reference heading and small changes for needle variations. The descent should be made at a reference rate of descent that is figured in advance, but the airplane must be at the MDA before it gets to the missed approach point if there is any hope of making a successful landing.

Visual descent points on some approach plates indicate the position beyond which a safe landing may not be made.

On a straight-in non-precision approach you must be careful that you don't attempt to dive at a runway that you locate when you are too close to it to make a safe landing. The missed approach points on those procedures are usually at the approach end of the runway or some other point on the airport itself, depending on what navaid is in use and where it is in relationship to the runway. If you are too slow to descend between the final fix and MDA, and find yourself breaking out right over the runway at approximately 400 feet AGL, it will be impossible to get down on most general aviation runways without running off the end.

Some approaches have visual descent points (VDPs) that are designated by the letter "V" on the approach plate. They indicate the position along the approach where the final descent to the runway can safely begin. Even if the pilot has the runway in sight

descent below MDA should not commence until passing the VDP. The VDP may be a mile or more from
the approach end of the runway and also represents the
point at which you should have the runway in sight if
you are to make a safe landing on it. Beginning a descent after the VDP will entail a higher than normal
rate of descent that could have an effect on where you
touch down on the runway and whether you can stop
on it or not.

On any non-precision approach to a straight-in
landing you should consider the performance factors
for your aircraft and decide at what point during the
approach you can no longer make a reasonable descent
and safe landing on the runway. It may be a mile from
the MDA, less, or more. For example, a Cessna 172
flying an approach at 80 knots will need less room to
descend to the runway and stop than will a cabin class
twin that flies the approach at 120 knots. The big flaps
on the 172 will increase the descent angle considerably, but still there is a point at which the airplane will
not be capable of descending the 400 or so feet from
the MDA to a short runway without running out of
room. You need to know how far from the MDA that
is, and if you see the runway after passing it carefully
consider any decision to attempt a landing.

Another difference between a precision and non-
precision approach is the need to level off at the MDA
instead of flying a constant descent to the runway. Just
before reaching MDA you need to add power and, if
necessary, make a pitch change to maintain the specified altitude. In level flight you must look for the airport or runway environment, but your first priority is
to fly the airplane. If you don't fly the airplane that
means it is flying you, and you probably will not like

the result.

Circling approaches demand a different discipline than straight-in approaches. All circling approaches are of the non-precision variety and I will discuss those in detail in the next chapter. There will be more on MDA and decision height (DH) in Chapter Nineteen.

Experience is the best teacher when it comes to instrument approaches. The more you do the better your approach work will be. But keep in mind that the legal minimum of six hours of instrument time and six approaches flown within the preceeding six months is not a personal standard. It is the minimum for everyone. Many pilots, especially those who don't fly IFR often, need more than that if they expect to fly an acceptable approach to minimums. Consider this. You get a flight instructor to give you an instrument competency check, then you don't fly IFR again for five months and 29 days. Legally you can go out and fly an IFR trip with approaches to minimums on the last day of your currency, but are you competent to do that? Probably not. Instrument pilots who don't fly on the gages regularly need to consider the weather they will fly in, what type of approaches they will use, and what the minimums will be. That is all part of one's personal limitations. If necessary they should get a safety pilot or instrument flight instructor to fly with them before going on a trip where their IFR skills might be tested.

Our ATC system is set up for professional pilots, but all pilots who use it must meet the standards the system imposes. That means having the capability to carry out whatever instructions, clearances, and approaches are assigned. If you are miles behind the airplane because you have not flown IFR for too long, you cannot use the system effectively. You can only cause delays for others, and problems for controllers and yourself.

CHAPTER THIRTEEN

CIRCLING APPROACHES

C ircling minimums for most instrument approaches are higher than those for a straight-in landing. It makes sense that an airplane that is going to overfly the airport or make turns from the final approach course to the landing runway should need extra maneuvering room. But too many pilots don't understand circling approaches, nor do they respect the minimums that are depicted on the approach plates.

Circling approaches are the most difficult, especially when the visibility is low. Visual illusions can easily fool pilots into thinking they are closer to or farther from the airport than they are. Pilots must keep the airport in sight during the maneuver, and that can mean a very tight turn to final for some high performance aircraft. You are obliged to maintain the MDA until you are in a position where descent to the runway is necessary. That depends on how close to the runway you are.

Most straight-in approaches offer circling minimums in addition to the straight-in minimums for the designated runway. That helps when a runway is closed or the winds on the surface are not aligned with the runway associated with the approach, but you cannot decide to circle to another runway after you have descended below circling minimums on a straight-in approach. If the airport you are landing at has only a single approach and it leads to a downwind runway you can circle to the other side of the runway. But you should begin the approach intending to land on the opposite side using the circling minimums as your MDA. If you intend to land straight-in, fly to straight-in minimums, and then decide to circle to the other side, you will bust your approach minimums.

An approach whose title designates a specific runway, for example, the VOR Runway 31 (see Figure 1), must have its final approach course aligned within 30 degrees of the runway. Any approach that is not so aligned is considered a circling approach (see Figure 2). The titles of those approaches are in the form of VOR A or NDB A. The letter changes depending on the number of approaches at an airport. There are no straight-in minimums for such an approach.

Occasionally an approach appears to line up with the runway but only circling minimums are offerred with it. One such approach is NDB A at the Fairfield

Circling Approaches 181

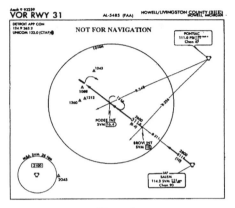

Figure 1
VOR RWY 31
Runway Alignment And Final Approach Course Heading Are The Same

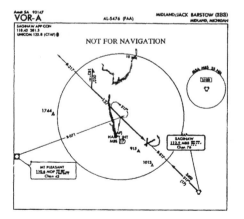

Figure 2
VOR A
Runway Alignment And Final Approach Course Are Greater Than 30
Degrees Apart

Airport at Hamilton, Ohio (see Figure 3). The inbound heading is 103 degrees and the runway direction is 110 degrees, but straight-in minimums are not authorized because of an abnormally high descent rate (more than 400 feet per nautical mile) required from the final approach fix, the Hamilton Beacon, to the runway. However, if the runway came into view far enough out to allow you to make a safe straight-in approach and landing, it is permissable to do so.

The workload on a circling approach is very high compared to other instrument operations.

Circling approaches can be dangerous if not flown correctly. Night approaches in reduced visibility require more skill, experience in dealing with various weather conditions, and understanding of what illusions can do to a pilot's visual perceptions. The workload on a circling approach is very high compared to other instrument operations, and pilots are often tempted to circle when visibility is not quite good enough.

A pilot who is flying under Part 91 of the FARs can begin an approach even if the weather is reported to be less than that needed for a successful landing. But there is little reason to do so when the known weather in the area is well below minimums, especially if the approach requires that the aircraft circle to land. If the known visibility is below landing minimums there is little hope of circling safely. Even if the pilot locates the runway while passing over it, if there is less than 1 mile visibility there will not be enough room to

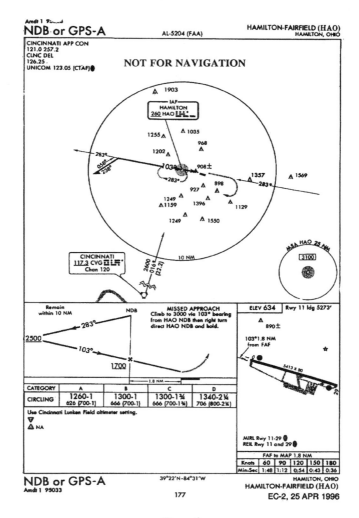

Figure 3
Circling Approach Only Though Aligned With Runway
Note Circling Minimums - No Straight-in Minimums

circle safely while keeping the airport in sight. It is not difficult to become disoriented while circling in low visibility, especially if visual contact with the airport is lost.

Minimums for each instrument approach are established for a reason. Terrain and obstructions require higher minimums, and a pilot who descends below them attempting to locate the runway or airport environment is begging for an accident. Yet, many pilots make a habit of trying to "duck under" the clouds by flying lower than the charted minimums.

I will not begin a circling approach unless there is good reason to believe it will be successful. For example, my home airport has several approaches. One is a VOR approach to Runway 31, and the other is the NDB approach to Runway 13. When I am coming from the west or northwest I often ask for the NDB approach when I know the wind favors the other runway. If I did not I would be in the air another 15 or 20 minutes by the time I got vectored beyond the airport, through some high density airspace, and back to the other approach.

I tell the controller that I am planning to fly the NDB approach to Runway 13 and circle to land on 31. But I will not even request a circling approach unless the automated weather observation system (AWOS) is reporting the ceiling at least 200 feet above circling minimums (439 feet AGL) and visibility of more than 1 mile. There is no point trying the approach with less than that.

A circling approach allows you to land on any runway at the airport providing ATC hasn't issued restrictions against doing so, but you must be careful to stay within the limits of the approach itself. Read the notes on the approach plate before beginning any procedure. One procedure may say that circling is only allowed on one side of the airport ("Circling south of Runway 27 not authorized") while another may restrict circling to one or more runways. Usually terrain or obstruction avoidance is the reason for such restrictions. If the visibility is low enough, and you fail to read the approach plate carefully, circling in the wrong direction could cause you to fly into the terrain on the wrong side of the airport, especially during a night approach in those conditions.

Plan on circling to a specific runway before beginning the approach.

      Another caution about circling. Plan on circling to a specific runway before beginning the approach, and when you locate the airport be certain that is the runway you are heading for. Many airport layouts are confusing. If you land on the wrong runway it could be shorter than you had planned and you could run off the end of it. You might land on a closed runway that could damage your airplane, or touch down on another active runway that other takeoff or landing traffic is planning to use.

      The type of airplane you are flying must figure into your planning whenever you decide to fly a circling approach. That is because the airspeed you fly on the final leg of the approach and the aircraft's proximity to the airport during the circling maneuver are critical to its success. If the visibility is 1 mile on the surface it could be less in the air. And how much room do you need in your airplane to circle to the runway? You should find out before attempting to do a circling approach to minimums.

Minimums on approach plates are broken down into aircraft categories, and are based on stall speed. The higher the stall speed of an airplane the higher the minimums because a faster airplane needs more maneuvering room. Be sure you know what category your airplane falls into and that you observe the minimums for it.

The higher your approach speed, no matter what category the airplane falls into, the more room you will need. But if you allow yourself to get too far from the airport you might lose sight of it, and you are then obliged to make a missed approach. But the circling maneuver should never be initiated unless the pilot is certain he or she has the necessary visibility to get to the landing runway without having to descend below the MDA until it is safe to do so. In fact, the descent from the MDA should not begin until the airplane is in a position to make a safe landing using a normal descent rate and normal maneuvering.

What is normal maneuvering? A 30-degree bank angle is the maximum recommended. If you need to use more you are too close to the runway and you could be inviting a stall/spin accident, especially if the visibility is very low.

A Piper Malibu pilot was vectored to an airport surveillance radar (ASR) approach to Runway 32 at Destin, Florida. Nine seconds after the approach controller told the pilot that he was at the missed approach point the pilot advised that he had the airport in sight and would be circling to land. Witnesses observed the aircraft fly over Runway 32 on a northwesterly heading at 150 to 200 feet AGL. Then the airplane made a 60- to 80-degree bank left turn back toward the airport. The airplane stalled, spun into some trees, and crashed to the ground. The two occupants were killed. The minimums for the straight-in approach to Runway 32 were 418 feet AGL while the circling minimums were 520 feet AGL.

The steeper the bank the higher the stall speed.

Remember from your student days that whenever an airplane banks the stall speed increases. The steeper the bank the higher the stall speed. A 60- to 80-degree bank angle so close to the ground is extremely dangerous, as we have seen in this accident, especially if the pilot is looking out the window at the runway and lets the airspeed decay. That should give you pause to consider why you need to maintain a reasonable distance from the airport during a circling approach, and that the minimum visibility that is required by the approach plate is absolutely necessary.

Several FAA inspectors told me during check rides over the years that they prefer to see the aircraft within 30 degrees of the landing runway before beginning the descent from MDA. But remember, your proximity to the runway affects where you start down if you don't want to overshoot.

Circling during an instrument approach is not like a VFR landing because if you are at the circling MDA you are at a much lower altitude than normal pattern operation requires, and the visibility is likely to be below VFR. At uncontrolled airports if you break out into VFR conditions while on the final approach course you must give way to any VFR aircraft in the traffic pattern.

I remember landing at an uncontrolled airport a few years ago and hearing the airport manager blast an instrument instructor and his student because they cut off a solo student in the traffic pattern. The weather was VFR and the pair were practicing approaches at a number of airports. They flew straight in to the runway and said they did not see the training aircraft on base leg. The airport manager told them that all VFR aircraft landing at his airport must fly the published traffic pattern. The instructor asked the manager how someone from his airport could learn to fly instrument approaches if they could not practice down to minimums. The manager replied that at that airport you flew the approach to pattern altitude, announced yourself while on the procedure and entering the traffic pattern, and broke off for a normal pattern. He did not want to hear any other method of practicing approaches.

That airport manager was concerned about student pilots in his traffic pattern, and he had a right to be. It was, and still is, a busy facility. Any time you are approaching an uncontrolled airport make certain that you do everything possible to avoid any conflicts with VFR traffic. If the weather is good plan on overflying a busy airport and entering the VFR traffic pattern if there is any evidence of other traffic in the pattern, or break off the approach as soon as you have the airport in sight and join the pattern in the normal manner. Another possibility is working out the arrival details with pilots of other aircraft that are on the unicom frequency. If everyone involved has each other in sight perhaps a safe straight-in approach can be made. But remember that some airplanes don't have radios. You must be alert for them. Safety must prevail, and if that means you fly the traffic pattern, so be it.

When I break out of the clouds into VFR weather I stop my descent at pattern altitude or above, depending on where along the approach course I am. Except in a training environment there is no need to circle to land at IFR minimums when you can make a normal and safer approach.

The circling approach itself is flown like any non-precision approach until you get the airport in sight. Then you must decide if you can land on the runway safely by circling at MDA. It is possible that you will be positioned directly over the runway with little forward visibility. If that is the case you probably don't have room to maneuver to one side of the airport or the other to land.

A circling approach in low visibility requires much of the pilot's attention inside and outside the aircraft. You must continue to monitor the flight instruments, especially the airspeed indicator and altimeter, while maneuvering visually. Don't begin to circle if there are not enough visual cues to do it safely. Use enough power to maintain your altitude and airspeed, but don't allow the airplane to fly back into the clouds. If you are flying a retractable, the landing gear should be extended at the final fix or before.

If you are flying a twin and lose an engine during the approach or the circling maneuver, the landing gear should be left in the wells or retracted again until the runway is made while other checklist items are dealt with. That will reduce drag while you are low and slow. If you lose an engine before commencing a circling approach do not attempt it. Find another airport that has a suitable straight-in approach (preferably with an ILS if the weather is marginal) and go there.

Sometimes pilots see nothing at
minimums and go searching for
the ground only to find it
before they want to.

Accidents often happen during approaches because pilots intentionally disregard legal approach minimums. Sometimes they get a glimpse of the ground and figure another 50 or 100 feet will get them below the clouds, while other times they see nothing at all at minimums and go searching for the ground. Too often they find it before they want to.

Some airports have only one instrument approach procedure, and when the wind is from the direction opposite the approach the pilot must circle to land. But he or she must have a good view of the runway before breaking off the approach for the circling maneuver and be certain that clouds are not lower on the other side of the airport. If the pilot loses sight of the airport or runway at any time he or she should make a missed approach.

CHAPTER FOURTEEN

THUNDERSTORMS

Thunderstorms are serious business whether you fly VFR or IFR. Associated turbulence, winds, rain, hail, and downbursts can cause heavy-duty problems even for pilots flying clear of the clouds. But if an aircraft gets inside a thunderstorm it will be a scary ride for the crew and passengers, and often results in damage to the aircraft.

When flying IFR in the vicinity of thunderstorms without detection equipment you must be cautious and alert. Work your way around the cells visually, staying clear of the clouds. If you can't do that you shouldn't be there. If you are in the soup you could fly into a

cell before you have the opportunity to turn away from
it. Sometimes it's possible to get vectors from controllers, many of whom have a Doppler overlay on their
radar scopes, but when you accept vectors and cannot
see for yourself what lies ahead you are effectively giving up a sizable portion of your command authority to
the controller. It's one thing to ask for vectors around
a small cell that lies in your path, but to rely on a busy
controller to vector you around heavy-duty weather is
something else entirely. You and your passengers
would be better served by sitting safely on the ground
waiting for the weather to pass.

Some older weather radars and lightning detection devices should no longer be used around serious
weather. Many first generation weather radar units are
no longer serviceable and may provide faulty indications of weather, or not see some cells at all. Whatever detection equipment you use, you should be totally familiar with how it operates. Just turning on a
weather radar and expecting it to show you where the
storm cells are can get you into trouble very quickly.

I told him I have never flown
through a thunderstorm

Several years ago I was interviewing for a
Captain's job on a Turbo-Commander when the
aircraft's owner asked me if I had ever flown through
a thunderstorm. I told him that I hadn't, though I had
come close a couple of times. I didn't get the job and
I'm sure the reason had to do with my answer to that
question. He interrupted me several times as the inter-
view went on and asked the question again. I gave him

the same answer each time. It was obvious that he didn't believe me.

At the beginning of the session he told me that he was searching for a new pilot because he was having problems with his present employee. One of the things the aircraft owner said he didn't like was flying through thunderstorms, and he acted as if it was a natural thing for any pilot to do. I have my doubts as to how many real thunderstorms he saw the inside of. Turbulence and rainfall in the vicinity of severe weather can give the impression of being inside a cell, and that is likely all he experienced. I didn't get the job because I told him the truth, that I have never flown through a thunderstorm. I felt that this guy was going to have more problems with anyone he hired if that was the criterion he was using.

When I started flying charter in the early 1970s, radars for light twins were just coming on the market. Their price was still out of the reach of most aircraft owners and charter operators. But the traffic levels were much lower than they are today, and controllers had more time to help pilots avoid weather. Still, you had to know who could help you and who couldn't. For example, center controllers couldn't see the storm cells very well on their radar scopes, while approach control radars gave a good indication of where they were but not their intensity. As time went on and the FAA changed to digital radar, weather was filtered out of the display, and only recently has the FAA added the Doppler capability to its system. But controllers in high density areas are very busy at peak traffic times and you should not rely on them to get you around severe weather. So, if you don't have detection equipment and know how to use it, stay away from severe weather.

I remember the first time I saw a large thunderstorm that was between my airplane and where I needed to go. I was riding in the right seat of a Cessna 310 during the early stages of getting checked out in it. The trip was from Reading, Pennsylvania to Hopedale, Massachusetts on a hot, humid afternoon in late June. We started the trip on an IFR flight plan though we were in visual conditions initially. Looking ahead we could see that before long we'd be in the clouds facing imbedded thunderstorms. We asked for a higher altitude but the controller couldn't let us climb high enough to let us remain in visual conditions. So the captain canceled the IFR flight plan and we climbed to 13,500 feet. At that altitude we could see the cells clearly and maneuver around them. The ride was smooth and the visibility excellent.

After landing we learned that
a tornado had spawned out of that
huge storm.

In the vicinity of the New York - Massachusetts border we saw one cell that was building so rapidly that it appeared to be exploding horizontally toward us. Looking up at it we could not see the top. We flew around the storm keeping our distance from it and eventually cleared it and the rest of the weather. When we landed at our destination we learned that a tornado had spawned out of that huge storm, which topped out at better than 70,000 feet. Since that day I have never seen a thunderstorm grow as rapidly.

The potential for danger around severe weather is high no matter what phase of flight the aircraft is in. Takeoff and landing can be extremely hazardous because of the constantly changing winds and the potential for a microburst out of the bottom of a thunderstorm cell. That's where severe downdrafts that are part of the internal mechanism of a thunderstorm "blow out" the bottom of it. As they strike the earth's surface they fan out in the 360 degrees of the compass. An aircraft attempting to take off or land in a microburst faces two dangers. One is from the core of the microburst itself, where the downdraft can be severe and cause an airplane to descend at a rate higher than it can climb, while the other is the instantaneous change in airspeed caused by a sudden change in wind direction. It is entirely possible for an aircraft to stall while flying at low airspeeds near the surface when a headwind suddenly becomes a tailwind.

A microburst is typically 1 or 2 miles wide, a small but very dangerous area for airplanes in the takeoff or landing phases of flight. The size of the aircraft doesn't matter. Many large jetliners have succumbed to this phenomenon with loss of life, and it is highly probable that many general aviation aircraft have as well. Unlike airliners, most general aviation aircraft don't have "black boxes" that record the effects of turbulence or wind prior to an accident, so we don't always know the exact circumstances that led to the crash.

Thunderstorm avoidance begins with your weather briefing. Do the forecasts along your route indicate severe weather activity? If so, is it of the air mass variety or the type associated with frontal activity?

Most of the time you can see air mass thunderstorms and visually maneuver around them. That is because they form from rising air currents provoked by the sun's energy. Usually there is no other weather associated with them. Sometimes air mass thunderstorms form in short lines and clusters, but normally they are easy to get around, though the activity may cover a wide area. You should give these storms a wide berth to remain clear of any turbulence or undetectable phenomena that may be associated with them.

Frontal activity is serious weather that you don't want to get involved with unless you have experience dealing with it and the airplane you are flying has the proper detection equipment. These storms can rise 60,000 or 70,000 feet into the atmosphere because they are fed with unstable air associated with two different air masses. Most of the time they are imbedded in weather systems and the pilot flying in the clouds cannot see them without a radar or lightning detection device. To be flying IFR in the vicinity of these storms without having the knowledge or the ability to determine where they are is to invite disaster.

The life of a thunderstorm consists of three stages. First is the cumulus stage, named for the type of cloud that gives birth to a thunderstorm cell, where moist, unstable air can be lifted in the atmosphere at rates of 2,000 to 3,000 feet per minute or more. Normally this maximum rate is reached late in the stage and at higher altitudes. The updraft lifts warmer air into the cooler atmosphere, and as it continues its ascent the moisture condenses and at some point it becomes supercooled water droplets and sometimes forms hail in larger storms.

*In the mature stage of a
thunderstorm, downdrafts can
reach velocities of 1500 feet
per minute.*

The cumulus stage gives way to the mature stage
when rain begins to impact the earth's surface, usually
10 to 15 minutes after the storm has risen above the
freezing level. The internal updrafts can reach velocities exceeding 8,000 feet per minute as the storm continues to draw more and more air from many miles
around it. Normally at some point between 25,000 and
80,000 feet the updrafts no longer support the amount
of water being gathered and it starts to fall out of the
storm. That action creates downdrafts as air is dragged
along with the heavy precipitation. These downdrafts
can reach velocities of 15,000 feet per minute. But
every storm has its limit and as the downdrafts increase
in intensity the updrafts weaken, bringing less "new"
moisture into the storm.

The storm is said to be in the dissipating stage
when the rain and downdrafts at the earth's surface end.
Air mass thunderstorms may last anywhere from 20
minutes to an hour while those associated with frontal
activity can last for hours. It is rare to find an individual storm cell that is more than 10 miles wide, but
the lines and clusters that form into "squall lines" can
extend for hundreds of miles in frontal activity.

So, while you are talking to the Flight Service
Station briefer or looking at your DUAT data, be alert
for any information concerning thunderstorms or severe weather. It might be found in terminal and area
forecasts, SIGMETS, Convective SIGMETS,

AIRMETS, center weather advisories, or in updates of current weather. There are several ways to deal with this type of weather, though most of them require waiting it out on the ground. And one thing you must realize is that forecasts are never 100 percent accurate. The Weather Service may believe that a cold front that is along your route will move through your departure point at a given hour, but that doesn't mean it will. It could come through sooner or later than the forecast time, and there could be severe weather before and after the front.

Keep that in mind as you formulate a plan to deal with frontal or air mass activity forecast to appear along your route. Depending on the length of the flight you may choose to fly a portion of it or stop for a few hours or overnight to allow the weather to pass through, then continue your trip. You might elect to take an alternate path around the weather. In Chapter Eight I described a flight where I flew north of my intended route, then west toward my destination to avoid some severe convective activity. If you have detection equipment you may decide to look at the weather and see if there is any safe way around it.

Before we get into detection devices let's discuss lightning. Most modern metal airplanes have little to fear from lightning because they are designed with bonding straps and static wicks that allow the electrical energy from lightning to dissipate off the trailing-edge surfaces of the wings or empennage. But that is not to say that the airframe will not suffer some damage from a strike. Composite aircraft are different because the construction material is an insulator instead of a conductor. These airplanes must have some sort of metal conductor embedded just below the surface of the structure if they are to dissipate electrical energy. Sometimes the conductor is a screen mesh and other times strips of lightweight metal. Pilots should fly homebuilt composite aircraft cautiously in the vicinity of thunderstorms because if they are not protected and are struck by lightning the integrity of the structure can be seriously compromised.

Still, lightning strikes are rare. A VFR-only light aircraft would have almost no chance of being struck during its life, and an airliner that is flown day in and day out in all kinds of weather is likely to take a strike a year.

Much of our knowledge of lightning and its effects on aircraft comes from research conducted by the U.S. National Aeronautics and Space Administration (NASA) in the 1980s during the emergence of new technology composite airframes, "fly-by-wire" control systems, and the installation of electronic flight instrumentation systems (EFIS) in modern cockpits. An F106B fighter aircraft was intentionally flown through selected thunderstorms at altitudes from 5,000 to 50,000 feet to discover why lightning struck an aircraft. Scientists discovered that 90 percent of the time when an aircraft was struck above 20,000 feet the electrical discharge was triggered by the airplane itself.

Sharp points on the aircraft concentrate and enhance the field surrounding the aircraft.

Static electricity is present in cloud formations and when an aircraft flies through a cloud it assumes the electrical potential of the cloud. Sharp points on the aircraft, such as wing tips, pitot tubes, propeller blades, and antennas concentrate and enhance the field surrounding the aircraft. The aircraft's movement through the field can increase its intensity as much as 100 times. As the aircraft's electrical potential continues to increase, the cloud's insulating properties start to break down and "leaders" are generated from the aircraft in search of charge pockets in the clouds. When one is found an electrical circuit is completed and lightning occurs. Although it is not impossible for an aircraft to become involved in a cloud-to-ground discharge, most of the time the "strikes" are of the cloud-to-cloud variety.

Since most general aviation aircraft fly at lower, warmer altitudes the chances for a random lightning strike are higher than for one triggered by the aircraft. Researchers also discovered that where there were a large number of lightning flashes in an area the chances for a triggered strike were reduced. That is because there were more direct paths for the electricity to take toward the ground than through an airplane.

So, in addition to the threat of turbulence, heavy rain, and hail in the vicinity of thunderstorms you need to think about lightning. I was flying a Cessna 310 some years ago when, on the approach to Providence, Rhode Island my aircraft was struck by lightning. I did not think so at the time, though the energy of the strike caused the King KN60 DME to malfunction, because I could find no evidence of it on the aircraft after I landed. But years later when I was researching lightning and described the event to Dr. Bruce Fisher, a research engineer at the NASA Langley Research Center in Virginia, he told me it was a strike. He said the DME would not have quit because of a close encounter with lightning. Had I looked very closely at the airframe I probably would have found a couple of pinholes where the lightning struck the airframe, probably on a leading-edge surface, and a couple more on a trailing-edge surface where it left the airplane. Since then I have seen pictures of airplanes that have been struck and often it is very difficult to detect the entry and exit points. That is why I did not see them on the 310. I did not know what to look for.

The closer you get to thunderstorm activity the more likely you are to encounter any of the phenomena I have described. Sometimes, though, they may be found miles from the core cell itself. So be sure you understand what you are letting yourself in for before beginning a flight that will take you near any thunderstorm activity.

Weather detection radar has been around since shortly after World War II. It has been upgraded over the years and today four-color radars reveal the location and intensity of precipitation. They are expensive units. If you are lucky enough to have a radar in your airplane it is probably an older version, perhaps a three-color or even a "green" screen. Whichever one you use, be certain you know exactly how it works and what it is telling you. It is easy to get into trouble around thunderstorm activity because of misreading the radar scope. Two DC-9 pilots did that in 1977 and flew into an area of severe rain and hail that destroyed both engines. The flight crew made an emergency landing in New Hope, Georgia that killed 62 of the 85 persons aboard the aircraft.

Lightning detection devices
and weather radar should be
used for avoiding weather,
not penetrating it.

Lightning detection devices are becoming more common in light general aviation aircraft because they take up little room in already crowded instrument panels. As with weather radar, some of the newer and more expensive versions are better than some of the older ones. Weather radar and lightning detection devices are two different technologies. Radar sees precipitation while a Stormscope or Strikefinder sees lightning discharges. The evidence of either should prompt a pilot to turn away from the weather to an area where no precipitation or lightning strike returns are observed. They should not be used for more than that. Trying to penetrate weather using either of these devices could lead you into a thunderstorm.

Both B.F. Goodrich and Insight, makers of lightning detection devices, agree that the best use of their products is in conjunction with a weather radar. When both devices are used together one has the benefit of more information. Radar signals are attenuated around intense storm cells, and it is possible that you may see a large cell in front of you with an apparent opening on one side of it and nothing behind it. But when you get around the other side of that storm you are likely to find another, perhaps more intense than the first, waiting for you. It might not be possible to avoid that one. That phenomenon is called "shadowing." The cell in front attenuates the transmitted radar signal so none of the signal penetrates it to find the second storm. That is what got the two DC-9 pilots.

But the lightning detection device, which is passive and doesn't rely on a transmitted signal, should see the lightning behind the first storm and warn you that there is something else there. If it doesn't show on the radar but does on the Strikefinder or Stormscope, you can bet shadowing is going on.

The reverse is also true. There can be lightning many miles away from the core storm itself. The lightning detection device displays it for you while the radar indicates there is no weather in that area at all. So using both devices together can make your job of avoiding weather easier. But remember that you want to avoid the weather, not penetrate it, no matter what combination of weather detection devices you have in your aircraft.

The key to survival around thunderstorm activity is to remain clear of it. Give yourself a wide berth around it, no matter if you are using a radar, lightning detection device, or your eyeballs to avoid it. Too many pilots thought they could beat the odds, and they lost. Summer IFR flying is not a game. It is serious business. Avoiding thunderstorms is easily accomplished by staying on the ground or landing in the face of them.

One summer I was flying a Piper Navajo from Pontiac, Michigan to Harbor Springs, a summer vacation spot about 180 miles north of the departure airport. When I departed Pontiac there was a small area of thunderstorms over the southern Upper Peninsula of Michigan that was moving to the southeast. It did not look like it would be a problem for me. About halfway through the flight pilots started calling Minneapolis

Center and asking for deviations around weather, and then they started looking for places to land. I could not see anything on my radar but the controller told me that there was some severe weather over the northern portion of the Lower Peninsula moving to the southeast at 50 knots. The speed of the weather caught my attention, because anything moving that fast is a force to be reckoned with.

My passengers were happy to be sitting this one out on the ground.

I landed at Houghton Lake to wait out the weather. The National Weather Service has a station on the airport and the meteorologists were kind enough to let me take a look at their weather radar. The small band of thunderstorms that I saw before I departed Pontiac was now a large area of very intense, severe weather bearing down on us. As the storms approached the airport it became apparent that my decision to land was right. The winds peaked at 60 knots during the 45 minutes or so that we waited for this stuff to move through. The rain came down in heavy sheets, like what you would expect in a tropical area, and my passengers were as happy to be sitting this one out on the ground as I was.

When the clouds started to lift and the sky began to brighten again I thought about moving on to our destination. I looked at the radar one more time, saw that the weather was by us, checked to see that the winds had settled down again, and loaded my passengers aboard the Navajo. The rest of the trip was uneventful.

The forecasts called for a slight chance of thundershowers that afternoon, but nothing like what we encountered. By the time I could see that weather on the radar I had already made my decision to land and wait it out, based on the reports the controller was receiving from other pilots plus his description of the speed of the squall line.

Thunderstorms are not to be trifled with because they can be a lot more than what you expect. Don't try to penetrate one, no matter what kind of equipment you are using or what type of aircraft you are flying. Give them a wide berth, and if you cannot do that turn around and get on the ground until they pass.

One more thing. Usually it is not the storm itself that causes an airplane to break up inside a cell. The way a pilot controls the aircraft in the updrafts and downdrafts usually determines how many pieces the airplane will be in when it exits the storm. The tremendous updrafts and downdrafts put such a strain on the airframe that any amount of overcontrolling can exceed structural limits. You should take precautions so you never get inside a thunderstorm, but if you should don't worry about your altitude. The updrafts and downdrafts will do that for you. Maintain level flight near maneuvering speed, if possible, with small movements of the controls.

Thunderstorms are probably the most difficult phenomena of nature that pilots have to deal with. While the mechanics of them are not difficult to understand, pilots do run into trouble operating around them. IFR pilots fly into them because they don't have the equipment to see them, and VFR pilots wind up in them because they did not pay enough attention to their weather briefings. Be certain you get a thorough weather briefing before departing, know where the weather is, keep abreast of changes, and if there is any doubt about your flight's proceeding safely around an area of severe weather, get on the ground first, then worry about how you are going to get to your destination.

CHAPTER FIFTEEN

ICING

Airframe icing is not something to play games with, yet many pilots do every year, and often they lose. The files are full of accident reports involving icing, and the experience level of the pilots involved ranges from low time to high time.

Some pilots who have de-icing or anti-icing equipment installed on their airplanes figure they can fly in the ice because of that gear. But the truth is that de-icing and anti-icing equipment on piston engine aircraft only buy the pilot a little more time to get out of the stuff. You cannot take off into icing conditions and expect to stay in them until you reach your destination.

Ice builds up on unprotected surfaces as quickly as it does on those that are protected. Even if you can remove all the ice from the wings, tail, and propellers, ice adhering to the airplane will slow it down and add weight while changing the aerodynamic shape of those surfaces. Because of the slower airspeed, you are in the icing conditions even longer, the added weight makes the aircraft less controllable, the stall speed creeps up with additional accumulation, and the potential for losing control increases the longer you remain in ice-producing clouds. Airplanes with no protection will ice up faster. Pilots know this, yet too often icing accidents involve airplanes with no de-icing equipment that should not have been flying under the circumstances.

Too often pilots disregard the portions of their weather briefings that deal with icing conditions. They listen to what the briefer says, but they don't hear it because they don't want to. Or they come up with an excuse to fly in icing conditions. I think the most popular one is that "there are no reports of it yet, so it is not there" followed by "I will climb right through the stuff and get on top."

Some pilots are under the impression that the FAA looks the other way when pilots fly in icing conditions without the proper equipment. But that is not so. There are any number of enforcement actions against pilots who flew in icing conditions, and the outcome for most is a sanction of some type, usually a license suspension.

The reason pilots get the wrong impression about the FAA's will to enforce the icing rules is because controllers don't usually turn pilots in even if they report icing. That is because they don't know which airplanes are certified for known icing and which are not. But if you get into an accident or have a problem that results in a reportable incident, or if an FAA inspector sees you land with ice on your unprotected airplane, you will undoubtedly be mailed a notice of violation.

The FAA considers any forecast for ice, or reported icing conditions, to be "known icing."

Another mistaken impression pilots have is that they can fly if icing conditions are forecast but not reported. That is not true. The FAA considers any forecast for ice, or reported icing conditions, to be "known icing."

Ice may not be reported because no one has yet to fly in the conditions. That happens often early in the morning between the time that the freight haulers have finished their overnight runs and normal daily flight activity begins, and at certain times on the weekends when there are lulls in activity. So, if you took off because no ice was reported, though moderate icing was forecast, guess what is likely to happen as soon as you get into the clouds and near the freezing level?

What is a "known-icing airplane"? It depends on how each type is certified. The flight manual for each airplane that is certified for flight in known icing conditions lists what equipment must be installed and operating before you can take off when icing conditions are forecast. For example, one manufacturer certifies its airplanes for flight in known icing with a complete de-ice/anti-ice package that includes wing and tail boots, electrically heated propellers, heated pilot windhsield, heated stall warning vane, heated pitot, and 100-amp alternators. Another includes in its certification wing and tail boots, electrically heated propellers, a heated pilot side windshield, heated pitot, ice detection light, heated stall warning transmitter, heater, and ice shields.

You can see some differences between the two manufacturers. One requires that the heater be operating and while the other doesn't mention it. Each airplane is certified differently, and you must check your flight manual to see if your airplane meets the known-icing requirement.

Some single engine airplanes are certified for known icing if the required equipment is installed and operating. The Cessna P210 is one, the Piper Malibu another, as are some single-engine turbo-prop aircraft. But most singles and many light twins have never been certified for known icing. Most single-engine piston airplanes lack the power to deal with icing conditions and a pilot who flies one that is certified for known icing must be very careful how he or she operates it when ice is present. Again, the equipment installed on the airplane really does little more than allow more time to find a way out of the ice. Don't ever believe that having de-icing equipment will allow you to fly through ice laden clouds indefinitely.

Now let's talk about how pilots work around icing conditions. Sometimes there is no way to avoid them except to stay on the ground. If you see reports of moderate to severe icing at the altitudes you normally fly, reported by large corporate jets or airliners, don't bother taking the airplane out of its hangar. That is more ice than any light general aviation aircraft can handle, including most that have de-icing or anti-ice equipment installed.

Jets normally climb and descend quickly through icing conditions. If the pilot of one reports moderate to severe icing over the short period that it is in the clouds think about how long you would be able to stay there and accumulate that kind of ice. How much ice is that?

The Aeronautical Information Manual identifies the levels of ice as follows:

1. Trace - Ice becomes perceptible. Rate of accumulation is slightly greater than the rate of sublimation. It is not hazardous even though de-icing/anti-icing equipment is not used unless the environment is encountered for an extended period of time (over one hour).

2. Light - The rate of accumulation may create a problem if flight is prolonged in this environment (over one hour). Occasional use of de-icing/anti-icing equipment removes/prevents accumulation. It does not present a problem if the deicing/anti-icing equipment is used.

3. Moderate - The rate of accumulation is such that even short encounters become potentially hazardous and use of de-icing/anti-icing equipment or flight diversion is necessary.

4. Severe - The rate of accumulation is such that de-icing/anti-icing equipment fails to reduce or control the hazard. Immediate flight diversion is necessary.

*Even when de-icing/anti-icing
equipment is used, there are
unprotected areas on the airplane.*

Look at the definition for moderate ice. The
words "potentially hazardous" should catch your attention. Even when de-icing/anti-icing equipment is
used, remember that there are unprotected areas on the
airplane where ice will build up. Prolonged flight in
these conditions can result in an accident.

Severe icing is not controllable by the de-icing/
anti-icing equipment. So, if you see or hear a report
from a jet, that does not stay in those conditions for
long, reporting moderate to severe icing in the clouds,
the reason why you should not venture into those conditions should be readily apparent.

Pilots need to be concerned about two types of
icing. Rime ice is a rough, milky, opaque ice formed
by the instantaneous freezing of small supercooled water droplets. And clear ice is a glossy, clear, or trans-
lucent ice formed by the relatively slow freezing of
large supercooled water droplets. Rime ice is milky
because air is trapped in the water droplet as it freezes
quickly on the airplane's surface. Clear ice is heavier,
accumulates more quickly than rime, and is harder to
get rid of. Both are very hazardous and pilots must
find a way out of icing conditions quickly whenever
they are encountered.

Freezing rain strikes an airplane and freezes like
clear ice. It gathers quickly and aerodynamically affects an airplane's flying characteristics to the point
where the airplane will no longer fly. It is extremely
dangerous and pilots should never take off in a light

general aviation aircraft when freezing rain is present. During the time it takes to taxi to the active runway and depart the airplane will become coated with ice and the result can be tragic. Also, the condition of runways and taxiways during freezing rain can make it a hazard just taxiing out.

Landing while freezing rain is present is almost as bad. The airplane descends into the colder air, where the freezing rain is present, from a warmer layer aloft. The rain freezes on the airframe on contact and builds up quickly. On landing the airplane is heavier and its aerodynamic foils are reshaped by the ice. That means a higher than normal stall speed, and the airplane may stall much earlier than the pilot expects it to. If a go-around becomes necessary the pilot will have his or her hands full and the maneuver may not be success-ful. Stopping on the ice-covered runway can also be a problem.

Sometimes icing conditions can be avoided by circumnavigating areas of weather that have an icing potential. Just how far out of your way you want to divert is the question, though. If the distance around the weather is too far, and that would depend on the airplane you are flying and its range, you are better off to delay your trip until the weather clears your route. Winter weather normally moves fast and with luck you will not have to postpone it more than one day, but if that is your decision you must sit it out until conditions improve no matter how long it takes.

Sometimes it is possible to climb through a thin layer of cloud to get on top and out of the icing condi-tions. But consider several things before you attempt that.

Light singles must be kept out of icing conditions because their rate of climb is slow even under normal conditions, and any ice adhering to the airframe will cause it to deteriorate quickly. So, if you get into the clouds intending to climb through the icing layers, they had better not be very thick. For example, if there is a cloud layer known to be 1,500 feet thick and you want to try to climb above it, do some homework first.

At a rate of climb of 500 feet per minute you will be in the clouds for three minutes. You can pick up a lot of ice in that time. Last year I was flying a Piper Navajo from near Detroit, Michigan to eastern Pennsylvania. While climbing to 9,000 feet between cloud layers I encountered some freezing rain that left a quarter to a half inch of clear ice on the airplane in less than 30 seconds. Fortunately the lightly loaded, de-ice/anti-ice equipped Navajo had the power to continue climbing and soon I was out of the stuff. But a light single could not have done that.

So what kind of icing clouds can you climb through in a single? Stay out of weather systems that may contain icing conditions. They seldom provide the opportunity for a single engine airplane to maintain itself without loading up quickly. The clouds you may successfully climb through are fair-weather types or thinner clouds usually seen after a weather system passes.

Years ago a friend of mine, a local flight instructor, and his student decided to practice instrument approaches in a Cessna 182 when icing was forecast to be in the clouds on the back side of a winter cold front. Someone asked Paul about the icing conditions and he said that they would go out and try an ILS. If they picked up any ice they would land out of the first approach.

They took off and flew the localizer outbound to the approach at our home airport. In those days there was no radar available and most approaches included a procedure turn. The intrepid pair completed the first approach with only a trace of ice and decided to try another. But a DC-9 was inbound so the two pilots had to climb to 4,000 feet and hold at the marker while the airliner landed. They noticed light icing accumulating and decided to fly the NDB approach to a full-stop landing as soon as the airspace became theirs again.

As they climbed they saw rime ice building faster on the airframe.

You know the old saying about the "best laid plans." On the NDB approach they descended to minimums and did not see the airport. The weather was deteriorating, and they had no choice but to go around and try the ILS approach. As they climbed away from the airport they saw rime ice building faster on the airframe.

Paul, the instructor, took control of the airplane. It felt very sluggish and he knew he was in trouble. Wisely he left the power set to the climb configuration as he leveled at 3,000 feet and flew outbound on the localizer. He made the procedure turn gingerly, expecting the airplane to stall at any moment, and as he approached the outer marker on the inbound leg it was obvious that he had to go to full power to keep the airplane in the air.

The ride down the glide slope was very demanding on Paul. The airplane was becoming harder to control as the flight continued. Finally, when they were very close to ILS minimums the student spotted the runway through a small hole in the ice adhering to the windshield, the result of hot air being pumped out of the defroster. Paul flew the airplane onto the runway touching down on all three wheels simultaneously before pulling the power back.

I have never seen an airplane with so much ice on it. Almost every surface was covered with at least an inch of rime ice. The tail tie-down was inches from striking the ground, the nosewheel almost fully extended because of the weight of the ice on the aft fuselage and tail surfaces. There was little doubt that this pair was lucky to survive their encounter with ice in the clouds. If they had not seen the runway they would have landed anyway whether they wanted to or not. The airplane would not have gone around again with the load of ice it had.

Remember that when you start thinking about climbing through a cloud layer to get on top when icing conditions are forecast or reported. You must be certain that you will get on top quickly. Then you must know that you will not encounter any more icing conditions before reaching your destination.

That is the key. If you see pilot reports that say the cloud tops are 3,000 feet and it is clear above, it might work if you are heading toward VFR weather. But if the reports indicate that the clouds are layered or if there is more icing reported along your route, stay on the ground.

Don't misunderstand me. It is not a good idea

to fly a light single, or any other airplane that does not have the proper equipment, in icing conditions. But pilots do it, often without thinking about the consequences. They don't use their heads and consider their options, nor do they pay enough attention to the conditions that exist before they take off. I hope that you will quickly learn that the times when you can safely fly an unprotected airplane in icing conditions are extremely rare, and that a great deal of thought must be given to the exercise before it is begun.

Be prepared to make a 180 degree turn.

Another thing to consider is that weather doesn't always do what we expect. If you think you will be on top of a layer of clouds containing ice all the way to your destination you have to be prepared in case it doesn't work that way. Be prepared to make a 180-degree turn to stay out of the ice laden clouds if you cannot outclimb them. If you are flying a normally aspirated airplane you cannot count on getting above 9,000 or 10,000 feet, and that is only if the airplane doesn't have any ice on it.

Many pilots don't use the 180-degree turn as a defensive measure during in-flight situations because they want to keep heading toward their destination. That is an easy way to get killed. Completing a flight safely is much more important than attempting to keep going toward the destination when some threatening weather phenomenon clearly is in the way.

One nearly 16,000-hour pilot found that out the hard way. Although he tried the 180-degree turn, he did it too late. He crashed a Cessna 172 about 22 miles south of Marquette, Michigan after it accumulated more ice than it could handle. The airplane departed the Chicago area at approximately 8:15 pm heading for Marquette.

The pilot checked the weather while enroute and was told that the Marquette weather featured an indefinite ceiling 100 feet sky obscured and a half a mile in fog. The temperature was 33 Fahrenheit and the dew point 31. The airplane continued to its destination and eventually Sawyer Approach Control told the pilot to descend from 4,000 to 3,600 feet for vectors to the ILS to Runway 8. Shortly afterward the controller issued a low altitude alert because the airplane descended below its cleared altitude, and the pilot told the controller, "Okay. we're going to have to make a one-eighty. We're going to have to get out of this ice. Sir, we are going to have to make a one hundred-and-eighty turn to the left."

Within minutes of that call the pilot declared an emergency and asked for an approach into Sawyer Air Force Base. He never made it. The pilot was seriously injured in the crash, two of the four passengers received minor injuries and the other two were not injured.

So, no matter what anyone tells you about experience, this pilot's 16,000 hours did not help him when he started accumulating ice. It should have told him not to fly that night when he got his weather briefing. There was a cold front located along the route and moderate rime or mixed icing was forecast for the entire route. Marquette was forecast to be 800 overcast and 3 miles, occasionally dropping to 300 hundred overcast and 3/4 mile.

If you own a twin that has de-icing equipment it still may not be certified for known icing. Back in the early 1970s the Cessna 310 I flew had wing and tail boots, hot props, and an alcohol windshield. It did not meet the standards for known icing aircraft because the windshield was not heated electrically and there was no vertical stabilizer boot. I understand that Cessna felt the stabilizer boot was not necessary, but the FAA disagreed. Starting with the 310R model, Cessna installed a vertical stabilizer boot.

So, if you own an airplane that has some de-icing equipment but is not certified for known icing, is it okay to fly in icing conditions? That depends. First, what is the age of the airplane and the de-icing gear? Has it been well maintained? Is it working properly?

Next, how much equipment do you have? Is your plane well equipped? Do you have wing and tail boots, heated or alcohol propellers, and a heated or alcohol windshield? Are the pitot tube and static source heated? That is the minimum equipment that you want to take off into known icing conditions.

Next, what icing conditions do you want to fly in? Most light general aviation airplanes that have de-icing equipment installed should never be flown in anything more serious than light to "occasionally" moderate icing. And when the ice starts building you must start looking for a way out. That could mean a higher altitude where you can get out of the ice-producing clouds or a lower one where the temperature might be warmer. You could also ask the controller if he or she knows of any altitudes that you could climb or descend to and be between layers. Another option if none of the others works is to get on the ground and sit out the weather.

If you want to avoid ice, you can.

Whether you are successful in avoiding ice or not will depend on your attitude. If you want to avoid it, you can. If you don't want to, you will not. It is those who don't want to avoid it that get into trouble. They don't say to anyone, "Hey, I'm going out to fly in the ice now." But they might as well. They are usually told when there is ice, and if the briefer makes a mistake and doesn't inform them, they should ask about it.

But some pilots feel the need to check out the conditions. Is it that they don't believe the briefers or the reports of icing in the clouds? No. They want to get where they are going, no matter what the weather. The only problem is that they don't tell themselves that in so many words. They fool themselves into thinking that they will turn back if things look bad. But often things turn very bad very quickly and they don't have time to think about turning back.

Are there times when icing is forecast to be in the clouds and it doesn't materialize? Sure. When that happens you will not see any reports of icing during the busy flying hours of the day. But remember three things. First, that forecast ice is known ice, whether it is there or not; second, that if no one is out flying there will not be any reports; and third, that the jets might go through light ice so fast that it doesn't accumulate, so no reports are generated.

If you go flying in the clouds and find there is no icing, you have little to worry about from the FAA. If there is no ice, it will be difficult for you to have an accident or incident related to it. And an FAA inspector who just happens to be at the airport you are landing at will not see your airplane covered with the stuff. But are you going to take the chance that there is no ice in the clouds when you launch, or are you going to use good old-fashioned common sense in making a reasonable go/no-go decision based on forecasts and reports? Whether you get into trouble with icing will depend on your attitude and judgment.

We have discussed icing in the clouds but now we need to talk about ice on the airplane before take-off. It can come from several sources. An airplane that is left outdoors during the winter is going to be covered each time there is a snowstorm. Often a broom or a brush is all that is needed to clean the stuff off, but if it rained before the white stuff started there could be a layer of ice under the snow. An airplane that collects ice during flight will need to be cleaned before it takes off on a subsequent flight, and one that taxis around in a wet or slushy environment could accumulate ice in the wheels or wheel wells, on the lower wings and control surfaces, and in pitot tubes and static sources.

Being certain that your airplane is free of ice before takeoff is a mandatory part of any preflight. And each pilot must be careful where he or she taxis. Water that freezes in the wheel wells or on the underside of the airplane can cause all kinds of problems after takeoff.

Four people were killed when a Mooney M20C

crashed shortly after departing St. Marys, Pennsylvania on a night VFR flight to Muncie, Indiana. The airplane had arrived at St. Marys earlier in the day, and when the pilot returned to the airport with his three passengers he noticed that frost had formed on the aircraft's external surfaces. He asked the line person if any de-icing solution was available, but none was. Witnesses watched the pilot and passengers try to scrape the airplane with credit cards, but the frost turned to ice. Finally, the pilot informed the passengers that it was time to leave and they all boarded the aircraft. The airplane became airborne and started its departure turn, then changed direction and started a descent at a 45-degree angle. It crashed in a wooded area about a half mile from the airport and burst into flames. The NTSB attributed the accident to the pilot's failure to ensure that the airplane was free of frost and ice before departure.

Ice in any form is one of the most serious hazards a pilot can face. It accumulates quickly and robs the airplane of performance and aerodynamic design. Your attitude will largely determine how you will deal with icing conditions and whether you will wind up having problems with it or not. Ice is not something to fool with. Be sure you know what you are doing when it is forecast or reported. If you get into it, no matter if you have a de-iced/anti-iced airplane or not, get out of it as quickly as you can. Avoidance is always the best measure, even it means sitting it out on the ground.

CHAPTER SIXTEEN

MECHANICAL DISCREPANCIES

AND EMERGENCIES

Whenever something unexpected happens while you are flying on the gages you will become distracted to some degree. How much of a distraction and what the outcome will be depends on your overall flying experience, proficiency, and currency in the clouds. I have repeated throughout this book that instrument flying is not easy, and probably the hardest day in any pilot's flying career is when he or she has a system failure and/or emergency when in the clouds. It can be tougher to handle than flying the low approach in very marginal conditions, especially when you consider that you might have to fly the same approach while attempting to deal with whatever has gone wrong.

The key to avoiding mechanical problems while airborne is good maintenance. If you own an airplane, take an active interest in its maintenance and be well versed on the state of its airworthiness. But how about rentals or other airplanes that you might fly? The pilot is always responsible for ensuring that the airplane he or she is to operate is airworthy, and to that end we preflight before starting the engine and check the systems before we take off. But mechanical difficulties, especially those related to poor maintenance, don't always show themselves until you are airborne, and if Mr. Murphy is aboard your airplane you can be certain that he will wait until exactly the wrong moment to show his fangs.

If you don't own the airplane you fly, chances are that you have little input into the depth of the maintenance that is performed on it. Some pilots don't know what good maintenance is, and too many aircraft owners conduct their maintenance not with safety of flight as the prime consideration, but the effect it will have on their pocketbook. It is one thing if they fly a poorly maintained airplane themselves, but when they rent it to others who have no knowledge of the true condition of the airplane, it would seem that some kind of fraud is being committed.

Again, the best way to avoid mechanical discrepancies that can lead to emergency situations in the air is to ensure that the airplane you are flying is well maintained. It is not that difficult to find a good mechanic who is thorough and conscientious. The price for his or her services will vary depending on whether

he or she works in a shop or alone, and the condition
your airplane is in at the outset will determine what is
needed and how much that will cost.

*Accidents resulting from inadequate
maintenance often involve catastrophic
failure.*

Accidents resulting from inadequate maintenance
often involve catastrophic failure that leads to an off-
airport landing. A Beech Sierra flown by an airline
transport rated pilot with 3,200 hours total flying time
departed Sarasota, Florida for Stuart, Florida on a VFR
flight. Witnesses told investigators that the airplane
climbed to an altitude of about 500 to 800 feet above
the ground when they heard a loud noise followed by
the cessation of all engine sound. The pilot transmitted a mayday while attempting to turn back to the runway. He was killed when the airplane stalled and spun
into the ground.

Investigators found that one of the blades separated from the propeller hub. That was the loud noise
the witnesses heard. They also noted that the airplane
had suffered two nose gear collapses in the previous 87
hours of flight. According to the aircraft log books the
hub was inspected and found to be serviceable. Yet
the NTSB blamed the accident on the failure of the propeller hub due to previous damage and inadequate main-
tenance/inspection following the prop strikes.

How would a pilot or aircraft owner know that
there was a problem with that hub? The only way to be
certain is to have a reliable propeller shop do the inspection. And even then a propeller involved in two

strikes over such a short period should cause anyone to be suspicious. Replacement of the propeller should have been considered.

I know of a Beech A36 that had its propeller separate from the airplane for the same reason. The crankshaft broke approximately 70 hours after an accident that severely damaged the entire airplane. The mechanic who did the repair work claimed he checked the crankshaft "according to the regulations," but others contend that he did nothing of the sort. The failure, which occurred on a very dark night, could have taken the lives of the three persons aboard the airplane, but the skill of the pilot and the proximity of an interstate highway saved them.

Mechanical failures are not only related to previous damage. That is why it is vital that you locate a conscientious mechanic to work on your airplane, one who is thorough and familiar with the type of aircraft you own. If you need a mechanic talk to aircraft owners, listen carefully to what they have to say about their mechanics, and choose accordingly. And always do a thorough preflight whenever accepting the aircraft after maintenance. Mechanics, like pilots, make mistakes, and much of the time they are evident during the walk-around.

It is difficult to come up with accurate statistics that indicate what percentage of accidents are caused by mechanical failure because often the accident itself is caused by the actions or inactions of the pilot-in-command following some kind of system failure. In other words the failure itself should not have been cause for the airplane's crashing.

Take, for instance, the Beech Sierra. When the

propeller separated the pilot declared an emergency and then tried to turn back to the airport at low altitude. He was killed because the airplane stalled and spun to the ground. That maneuver is often attempted by pilots who lose their engines at low altitude and often the result is the same. Was the fatal accident the result of the propeller hub failure or did it occur because the pilot tried to turn back to the airport? Most experts agree that a straight-ahead landing is preferable in those circumstances than the 180-degree turn to the runway. If he had not made the turn he would have had to make an off-airport landing, but I believe the accident would not have been as severe.

So, not all mechanical failures are responsible for the accidents that result. That is particularly true of those that occur while flying on the gages. A Piper Turbo-Arrow crashed at Radium Springs, New Mexico following a vacuum pump failure. The pilot reported the loss of her attitude indicator to ATC, said she was IMC, and that she "was in trouble." That was the last transmission received from the aircraft. It was a dark night with snow reported at 10,000 feet, the Arrow's cruising altitude. The pilot's log book indicated she had 1,482 hours total flying time, 12 hours in the Piper Arrow, and 107 hours of instrument flight. However, this was her first known flight in actual instrument conditions.

Should the loss of a vacuum pump in IFR conditions result in an accident? Not if the pilot is proficient at flying partial panel. The problem is that we suffer so few failures these days that too many of us don't maintain adequate currency without our vacuum-driven instruments. The NTSB blamed this accident on the failure of the vacuum pump, the dark night, the snow, the pilot's loss of control, and her inexperience in flying in actual instrument conditions.

In another accident a Piper Aztec departed Teterboro, New Jersey for Pittsburgh. The departure weather featured a 500 foot overcast ceiling and 3 miles visibility. The departure controller cleared the aircraft to 4,000 feet, and the pilot acknowledged the transmission while climbing through 1,800 feet. The aircraft reached 2,800 feet before starting a descent to the ground. A witness observed the airplane in a spin just before it crashed.

Investigators tore the left engine down and discovered that two of six fuel injector nozzles were restricted. The aircraft's logs indicated that the last time the injectors were cleaned was eight years before the accident. The manufacturer of the fuel injection system recommends that they be cleaned during every annual inspection or each 100 hours of flight. Additionally the airplane was 188 pounds over its maximum allowable gross weight, and the center of gravity was 1 inch aft of the aft limit.

The NTSB blamed the accident on the inadequate maintenance and inspection of the fuel injector system, resulting in a partial loss of power to the left engine. While that may have begun the sequence of events that resulted in the accident, it seems that the pilot's failure to keep the overloaded airplane flying was the real reason for the crash. The NTSB called that a contributing factor.

Why was the pilot unable to keep the airplane flying? Was he so distracted by the partial power loss that he forgot to monitor his instruments? He should have stopped the climb when he realized that he had a power loss and tried to maintain altitude. If four cylinders were still operating it would seem likely that level flight or at least a controlled descent could have been sustained while the pilot returned to the airport or another one nearby. But he probably was concentrating on the power loss more than flying the airplane, and he may have been trying to keep the airplane climbing in accordance with his clearance. Another possibility is that since he did not know the nature of the engine problem he pulled the left throttle back to idle hoping to save the engine from catastrophic failure. But if he did that he never feathered the propeller, and that could have contributed to his loss of control.

While we don't know the exact sequence of events that caused the pilot to lose control of the Aztec, we do know that he failed to keep his airplane flying. That is the number one rule in any situation facing a pilot, whether flying VFR or IFR. No matter what the failure is, even if it rates emergency status, fly the airplane before all else or you are likely to come spinning out of the clouds like the Arrow and Aztec pilots did.

Even ordinary events during flight can cause distractions that result in loss of control.

Anything, even ordinary events during the flight, can cause distractions that result in the loss of airplane control. The pilot is responsible for prioritizing everything that occurs in the cockpit, much as a computer prioritizes which instructions it will execute first.

Keeping the airplane in the air is always the first item on the agenda. If a pilot does not do that there is little need for him or her to do anything else, because he or she is just along for the ride.

Let's look at some distractions that cause pilots to forget to fly the airplane. Some of them are simple but very effective. For example, copying a clearance while airborne is a major distraction for instrument pilots because they must take their eyes off the instruments to write the clearance on their log. The most effective way to copy a clearance in the air is to turn on the autopilot while you are too busy to hand fly the airplane. But many light singles and some twins don't have autopilots, and even if your airplane has one installed, using "George" does not relieve you of the responsibility for making sure the airplane is doing what it is supposed to do. It just makes the physical act of copying the clearance easier and the ride more comfortable for the passengers.

If you don't have an autopilot you must have an established method of writing with one hand and one eye, while the other hand and eye is devoted to keeping the airplane in the air. Sounds difficult and it is, but you cannot stop flying the airplane to copy a clearance. If you are busy when ATC calls with the new clearance tell the controller to stand by. Don't rush to copy the clearance if it will affect your flying. Wait until you have the time.

Passengers are another source of major distractions, especially the one sitting in the seat next to you who wants to talk constantly. You must be firm with your passengers and explain to them before the flight begins that you need to concentrate on your flying. Too much noise in the cabin is distracting, and that can lead to an accident.

But the majority of distractions during instrument flight that cause accidents come from system failures such as the those I have described. A VOR may not seem to work properly and the pilot spends too much time trying to find the cause instead of using the number two. That can occur right after takeoff at the busiest time of the flight. The best thing to do is use the number two and wait to troubleshoot the number one until you are at cruise altitude, the airplane is reconfigured, and you have the time to devote to it. Most of the time you will find that you selected an incorrect frequency before takeoff, or that you neglected to set it at all.

In Chapter Five I described how a directional indicator had failed in a Cessna 402 I was flying, causing the autopilot to fly the airplane in circles. I was looking at the chart when that happened, and when the controller called me to ask about my heading I told him we were on course. I did not even look at the instruments, allowing the chart to distract me from watching the progress of the airplane instead.

Another distraction that occurs during instrument approaches is the failure of the landing gear to extend properly. The reasons for that vary and most of the time simply recycling the gear will solve the problem. But when do you put the gear down? I usually extend it just as I am intercepting the glide slope on a precision approach or near the final fix on a nonprecision approach. If anything is going to go wrong it will be at that point, a very critical one where the approach must be stabilized and the pilot's attention devoted to the instruments. If you recycle the gear once at that point and it does not solve the problem there is no point continuing the approach.

Too much is at stake for a pilot to keep flying the approach while trying to troubleshoot the landing gear. He or she is too close to the ground and getting closer every second. That is a very dangerous place to be with your attention divided between flying the airplane and trying to fix the gear problem.

The controller will issue holding instructions or assign you airspace where you can figure out the problem.

There is no need to declare an emergency because the gear did not extend properly on the initial try, but after recycling it once with the same result tell the controller that you need to find a place to troubleshoot it. He or she will issue holding instructions or assign you a block of airspace where you can figure out the problem with the system.

If it is necessary to manually extend the landing gear you are likely to need more time to pump or crank it down than what is available between the final approach fix and DH or MDA. And that does not include the time required to troubleshoot the system before deciding that manual extension is necessary. Don't attempt to deal with a malfunctioning gear system on final approach. Talk to the controller and get some distance between you and the ground. But remember, while you troubleshoot the gear at altitude you still need to fly the airplane.

Many gear-up landings are caused by the failure of the pilot to lower the landing gear. When that happens the pilot has usually become distracted from the normal sequence of events during an approach. It can happen in VFR or IFR conditions.

Normally landing with the gear up is not an accident where the passengers or pilots get hurt. But in one case the pilot of a Beech A36 realized as the propeller touched the runway that he had forgotten to extend his gear. Witnesses watched the airplane become airborne again, climb to about 30 feet AGL, then descend in a left bank. The airplane cartwheeled when the left wing contacted the ground and the pilot was killed.

Could this happen to you? The Beech pilot probably reacted instinctively when he realized the gear was not down. But he saw it too late, and he should have let the airplane settle to the runway. Once the propeller struck the runway it was too late to go around. Investigators did not find evidence of engine failure because of the prop strike, but the airplane's speed was probably much too slow to abort the landing.

It is not that difficult to fixate on the instruments during an approach, especially one to minimums. If anything unusual occurs, such as a controller asking you to maintain a higher than normal airspeed to the marker, your routine can be interrupted. It is imperative that you include another check of the aircraft to ensure that it is in the landing configuration sometime before leaving DH or MDA to avoid landing gear-up or finding yourself in the situation the Bonanza pilot faced.

Pilots must balance the utility of their airplane against the potential for a system failure or emergency.

For example, I received a letter from a pilot who read an article I wrote in which I said I would not fly my Piper Arrow across Lake Erie on a westbound flight. He asked me, "Why is it considered unsafe to fly across a body of water if that is the shortest distance (time) between two points?" I responded that I elected on that day to avoid the water exposure because my altitude was low (3,000 feet) and I did not want to be beyond a point where I could make it to land if my engine quit.

I explained further that I have flown the same airplane eastbound across Lake Michigan at 9,000 feet on an IFR flight plan. Experiencing a normal westerly wind my exposure time over the middle of the lake was very short.

Each time we fly we must consider the potential for a catastrophic failure and leave ourselves a way of dealing safely with one. Does that mean I don't have faith in my airplane? Absolutely not. But playing "what if?" is a part of any pilot's job.

For example, the last thing any of us wants to experience is an engine failure in a single engine airplane while on an IFR flight. If it should occur while we are flying over an area where there is no ceiling or visibility because of low-lying fog, what can we do? Not much. So, would you fly your single engine airplane over an area where you had nowhere to go if the engine quit? What most pilots do is balance the odds of something happening to them against the conditions they are faced with and make a decision that is appropriate for their experience level.

We could prevent all system failures and emergency situations if we did not fly our airplanes, but that is a drastic action to take when only a small percentage of pilots and airplanes are affected each year. Each of us can limit our exposure by ensuring that our airplanes are well maintained and that we use our heads when planning and piloting our flights. Always leave yourself an out in case you do have a problem. And keep yourself current on emergency procedures, especially flying with only a partial panel.

In my 26 years of flying I have never declared an emergency, but I would not hesitate if the situation demanded it.

In my 26 years of flying I have never declared an emergency, though I would not hesitate to if confronted with a situation that demanded I do so. But I have only encountered one true emergency situation in all that time. I was 6 miles away from the non-controlled airport I was going to land at when the right engine on the Cessna 421 I was flying quit due to a frozen fuel control valve. There was plenty of fuel aboard the airplane. I feathered the engine and instead of flying the normal traffic pattern, I landed out of a straight-in approach. Fortunately there was no other traffic in the area at the time. In that situation calling a controller and declaring an emergency would not have done anything for me, but in most other situations where an engine fails I would not hesitate to do that.

I attribute my lack of experience with emergencies not to luck or even skill but to the fact that the airplanes that I have flown over the years have received quality maintenance. I have never engaged a mechanic who specializes in "fifty dollar annuals," nor have I skimped on replacement parts, though I have often cringed at some of their prices.

That is no secret that I am sharing with you. If you were to ask others who have been successful over the years about their experiences and reasons behind their lack of difficulties, I think they would say the same things. Good maintenance and a good head on your shoulders are the best tools for survival in the world of instrument flying.

CHAPTER SEVENTEEN

THE NON-RADAR ENVIRONMENT

In the early days of airline operations there was no ATC. Often pilots flew in the clouds with no assurance that another airplane was not bearing down on them, one flight crew just as blind as the other. But in those days there were not that many airplanes flying, certainly not as many as today when, depending on the weather, there could be thousands of airplanes aloft at any given time. The chances of a midair occurring enroute were slim, though like today, approaching an airport could be dangerous if more than one airplane sought the runway at the same time.

The first step in any sort of traffic control was

the attempt by the major airlines of the day to keep track of the comings and goings of the airplanes in their own fleets. Seldom was information passed between the airlines, but at least pilots knew if there was more than one airplane from that airline in their vicinity. Eventually the government took over control of all IFR aircraft and began what has evolved into our modern ATC system.

Today pilots enjoy radar coverage across much of the continental United States. The gaps in coverage are becoming fewer, but some exist. Also, when a radar facility goes down because of faulty equipment or periodic maintenance pilots and controllers may need to revert to non-radar operation. Non-radar operations occur so infrequently that most pilots, and some controllers, have problems when called on to work in that environment.

Today's radar systems are coupled with computers that reduce the controller's workload considerably compared to the 1950s and 1960s. In those days "shrimp boats" were manually pushed along the track of an airplane under ATC's control. A paper or plastic tag was attached to it so the controller would know what target the blip on the screen represented. I remember when I took a tour of the Boston Air Route Traffic Control Center as a teenager and watched the controllers move the sailboat like pieces along the blips on their table-mounted radar scopes. Today the data tag is computer driven and follows the target automatically. If that computer goes down a busy controller gets much busier very quickly, like a pilot who loses his or her vacuum pump and has to fly using a partial panel. If a controller is not proficient at operating without his or her computer generated tags, or without the radar, traffic separation standards can be breached quickly, putting many pilots and passengers in jeopardy.

A controller who cannot see the airplane on radar relies on pilots' position reports.

Pilots may create the same hazards in a non-radar environment if they are not cautious or don't understand what is required of them. A controller who cannot see the airplane on radar relies on pilots' position reports to separate traffic, and if those reports are not accurate conflicts can occur. If a pilot wanders off course in a non-radar environment it may go uncorrected until the pilot realizes that something is wrong. If uncorrected, the airplane might run into high terrain in an area where it was not supposed to be, or venture into the protected airspace of another airplane. When there is no radar a check valve is missing and pilots' awareness of what is going on around them must be at a higher level.

In the radar environment we seldom hold any more because controllers can vector airplanes to follow each other instead of stacking them up over fixes, but when you want to land at an airport that is not served by radar, or during hours when the radar facility is not in operation, you could be assigned to a holding pattern while others ahead of you fly the approach.

Often when there is no radar a pilot is required to fly an entire approach, another thing that he or she does not do very often. That means that either a course

reversal in the holding pattern is required or a procedure turn must be flown. That is more work for the
pilot because he or she must monitor position and altitude carefully so the airplane is kept within the approach airspace.

If you have not practiced holds recently the non-
radar environment during IFR conditions is not a good
place to do so. When you are issued a holding clearance you must keep the airplane within the protected
airspace for several reasons. There may be high terrain in the vicinity or other airplanes holding in adjacent airspace. If you allow the wind to blow you out
of your protected airspace or if you simply wander out
of the hold you are putting your aircraft, and possibly
others, in jeopardy.

Remember that when you fly IFR in a radar
environment controllers watch your position relative
to high terrain, but when you are out of radar contact,
it is your responsibility. You must monitor your position and know that your altitude is high enough to clear
any terrain or obstacles along your route.

If you are flying an approach be certain you
study the procedure thoroughly and understand where
the terrain is in relation to it. Back yourself up using a
radial of a VOR or bearing from an NDB that you don't
want to cross under any circumstances in the event the
terrain nearby is higher than you are flying. A GPS or
Loran is a good tool that can keep you apprised of your
exact position in relation to the approach and the terrain.

You should always be familiar with the location
of nearby terrain during any approach, whether radar
is available or not. But in a non-radar environment

there is no one to back you up if you make a mistake, so you must be certain by continuously checking and cross-checking your position that you are exactly where you want to be. There is no room for error.

A commuter flight approaching the Shenandoah Valley Regional Airport in Virginia crashed into the side of a mountain after Washington Center terminated service as the airplane descended below radar coverage. When investigators simulated the flight in another airplane they found that by leaving their VORs selected to the Montebello VOR instead of resetting them to the Shenandoah Valley localizer they flew over the crash site.

The ILS approach is to Runway 5 (see Figure 1). The aircraft was coming from the northeast across the CEROL Intersection. A radar plot shows that the aircraft made a procedure turn but did not intercept the localizer inbound. Instead it continued to fly a 75-degree heading until it no longer showed up on radar. The crash site was located on the Montebello 045-degree radial. The inbound heading on the localizer is 045 degrees.

The NTSB concluded that the most likely scenario was that both pilots failed to switch their nav radios from the Montebello VOR to the localizer after passing the CEROL intersection. The lack of positional awareness on the crew's part probably led to the accident.

There probably were other indications in the cockpit that the airplane was not where it should have been. The ADF was most likely tuned to the Staut localizer outer marker (LOM) and indicated that the airplane was east of the proper course. In fact, inves

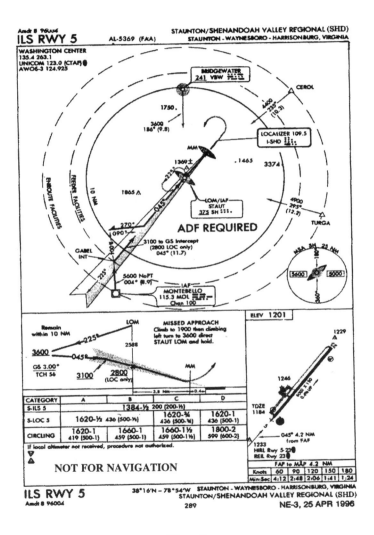

NOT FOR NAVIGATION

Figure 1

tigators felt that the flight's Captain might have noticed that and was trying to climb when the aircraft hit the mountain.

In a non-radar environment, there is no one looking out for you except you.

In a radar environment the Washington Center controller would have vectored the airplane to final approach and would have seen it continue through the localizer and so advised the crew. That report would have caused the pilot to check his equipment, and he probably would have caught the error. But in a non-radar environment there is no one looking out for you except you. Your situational awareness must be high at all times.

A few years ago I was flying a Cessna 421 from Marathon, Florida to Key West. The weather at Marathon was VFR, but it was IFR at Key West with an overcast ceiling at 600 feet and a visibility of 1 mile. There were moderate rainshowers moving in from the west and southwest.

I took off VFR from Marathon knowing what the weather was. I had an IFR flight plan on file and called Key West Approach for it shortly after becoming airborne. The controller issued me a clearance via radar vectors and gave me a heading to fly that would keep me clear of the restricted area that lies to the northeast of the airport. I was told to expect the VOR/DME approach to Runway 27.

When I tuned in the VOR I got nothing. I immediately tried it again using the number two nav radio and got the same response. I reported it to the controller, and then the pilot of another aircraft that was inbound also advised that he was not receiving the VOR. The controller did not respond right away. I assumed he was trying to find out what the problem was.

Finally the controller came back on the air and said, "Five Alpha Mike, I've lost radar contact with you. Our radar just went down." I sat up in my seat trying to think ahead of the controller. I had no VOR to navigate to and he had no radar. He had other airplanes inbound but I had no idea where they were. I reviewed the approach plates for the airport and found that in addition to the VOR/DME approach that I was expecting to fly there was an approach using the Fish Hook NDB 1.2 miles west of the airport.

My first guess was that the controller would tell me to proceed to Fish Hook and hold while he tried to sort things out. I waited for that clearance for a couple of minutes and during that entire time the approach control frequency was silent. Finally the controller came back on the air with an off-the-wall question.

"Five Alpha Mike can you hold in your present position for a few minutes?" he asked. That was totally unexpected because the controller had no idea whether I was in IFR or VFR conditions, nor did he know precisely where I was because so much time had passed since the radar failed. I was still VFR so I answered in the affirmative and started orbiting right where I was. I could have held my position using a bearing off Fish Hook and timed turns in a hold if I had to, but that was not necessary. The controller told me to maintain my position and he would let me know when he got the radar back. He dealt in a similar fashion with the other two airplanes that had been inbound when the radar went down. I was not issued an expect-further-clearance time.

I was perfectly safe because I had good visibility where I was and could have turned around and gone back to Marathon at any time, but I had to wonder about how that situation was handled. It seemed like the controller did not know what to do when the radar failed. Perhaps there was more to it than I understood. I was not there with the controller and did not know what was happening on the ground, but I did expect the situation to be handled much differently than it was.

Several minutes later a new voice came up on the approach control frequency and told me the radar was operating again and that I was in radar contact. The new controller vectored me for a surveillance approach to Runway 27 at Key West. The approach went smoothly and soon I was on the ground.

If you are a student instrument pilot ask your instructor to take you on a cross-country where you will encounter non-radar operations. If you are a current instrument pilot and have never worked in a non-radar environment find an airport where you can practice approaches without help from ATC. Any airport that has an instrument approach but does not have radar coverage from the minimum enroute altitude down to the surface will work. If you cannot locate anything nearby there should be an airport where the tower and approach control close late at night. Or, with ATC's help you and your instructor could simulate a non-radar environment by flying an enroute leg to an initial approach fix (IAF) and a complete approach.

If there is high terrain nearby make certain you will be alerted if you are drifting toward it.

When you are faced with a non-radar approach be certain that you review the instrument approach plate carefully. Trace the route you will take from the IAF and follow the approach to its conclusion. Be sure you understand exactly where you are to leave one altitude and arrive at the next. And if there is high terrain nearby make certain you will be alerted if you are drifting toward it by reference to a VOR radial, NDB bearing, or some other fix that you don't want to cross.

Before beginning any approach cross-check your instruments and make sure everything is set correctly and that all appears normal. Any time you feel something is not right abandon the approach, get some altitude, be certain you are clear of the terrain and other obstacles, then search for the cause of your uncertainty. And above all else, remember to fly the airplane first.

Flying in a non-radar environment increases the workload for instrument pilots, especially when holding patterns and complete approaches are necessary. In most of the country the only time you will be forced to work in a non-radar environment is when the ATC equipment fails or if you fly late at night after a radar approach facility closes. If the radar fails unexpectedly you could be caught off guard, and if you fly late at night you might be fatigued and slow to react or understand that you are not where you should be, since there is no controller to advise that you are drifting off course.

If you have problems in the radar environment

with staying ahead of your airplane they will be worse in the non-radar world. Here you must do all the thinking for yourself, and long before the airplane gets to the point where there is a change to be made. Controllers will call you continuously asking for position reports so they can keep other airplanes' expect-further-clearance times current. And if you are forced to make a missed approach, you will fly the published procedure instead of being radar vectored around for another approach.

    If you fly enroute in a non-radar environment you are required to make periodic position reports. Looking at your IFR chart you will notice the solid triangles (see Figure 2) that appear along the Victor Airways. Those are mandatory reporting points. It

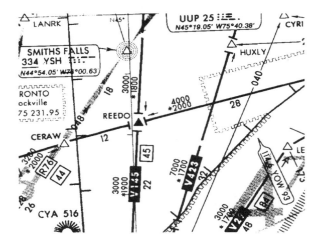

Figure 2

seems as though there are fewer of them now then there have been in the past, but with radar coverage extending across the continental United States they are seldom used as originally intended. Some instrument pilots may not remember what that symbol means because they have never flown outside the radar environment.

Too many of today's pilots rely on radar for a myriad of functions from providing IFR separation to learning from the controller what their present position is. Most of us grew up in the radar environment and don't know how to function outside it. There's little published about operating in the non-radar environment but each of us who flies on the gages must be familiar with the procedures before we hear the words "radar contact lost."

CHAPTER EIGHTEEN

LEGAL ALTERNATES

Many instrument pilots don't understand the pre-requisites for a legal alternate. There is confusion in differentiating the need for an alternate with existing or forecast weather conditions and other requirements that determine the selection of one. And fewer pilots understand that once they are airborne the whole alternate exercise can be completely disregarded if one is inclined to do so. It is strictly a preflight activity. All that is required of a pilot is to specify an alternate airport in the flight plan to show that in the planning stages an alternate landing site was available. In the air the pilot is to use his or her best judgment in the conduct of the flight.

The best instrument pilots always have a way out of any situation that may arise, and that includes knowing what they would do if the weather or some other factor suddenly forced a change to their plans for landing at the intended destination. So, even if the requirement for an alternate ends at liftoff, a good pilot will regard an alternate landing site mandatory during all stages of the flight.

It is not difficult to identify, during your flight planning stage, airports along the route that you could divert to if unforeseen weather forces an early landing. As the flight progresses you can keep track of the weather at these airports as well as at your original destination and alternate.

What are the legal flight planning requirements for an alternate? The first thing you have to determine is if one is necessary. FAR 91.169 (See Appendix A) is the rule that deals with IFR alternates, and it requires an alternate except when the intended landing airport has an instrument approach procedure available "and for at least one hour before and one hour after the estimated time of arrival, the weather reports, forecasts, or any combination of them, indicate - (1) that the ceiling will be at least 2,000 feet above the airport elevation; and (2) the visibility will be at least 3 statute miles." Notice that if you file an IFR flight plan to an airport that does not have an instrument approach you must file an alternate no matter what the weather forecasts indicate.

That is straightforward, or is it? What if the forecast for the destination calls for a 2,500 foot broken ceiling, 5 miles visibility, and an occasional 1,500

foot ceiling and 1 mile visibility? Any time the forecast indicates the ceiling may be below 2,000 feet and
the visibility less than 3 miles you must file an alternate in your flight plan.

If you suspect the forecasts are wrong what
should you do? For example, the forecast for your
destination projects a ceiling of 5,000 overcast and 5
miles with an occasional 2,500 foot scattered and unlimited visibilities. Yet when you check the current
weather you find the station reporting 1,500 overcast
and 2 miles in fog. The wording of the FAR covers
that situation because it tells you to rely on "the weather
reports or forecasts or any combination of them." In
other words a current weather report for a destination
that is less than an hour away from your starting point
that indicates that the weather is below 2,000 and 3
requires an alternate even if the forecast suggests the
weather should be better.

*The period you are concerned with
is one hour before to one hour
after scheduled arrival.*

The period you are concerned with is one hour
before to one hour after scheduled arrival. A strict
reading of the rule allows you to take off on a two-
hour flight without filing an alternate if the reported
weather is below 2,000 and 3, provided that it is forecast to be above that for the hour before and hour after
your scheduled arrival. Is that a wise thing to do? It
depends on several things. Let's look at a hypothetical
situation.

You are flying from Detroit, Michigan (DET)

to Lexington, Kentucky (LEX). You are planning 2 +
10 enroute with a scheduled departure time of 7 a.m.
The forecast for Lexington is for 10,000 scattered to
broken with 5 miles visibility in haze for the period
from 8 a.m. to 10 a.m. Just before departure you check
the current weather and find that Lexington is reporting 1,000 overcast and 1 mile in fog. You check to see
if the forecast for Lexington has been amended and find
that it has not.

You look at the area forecast and find that generally improving weather is forecast as the morning fog
burns off. You decide that the forecasts are accurate
and that you don't need an alternate as you begin your
flight. In this instance you have complied with FAR
91.169 and determined that no alternate is necessary.

If, on the other hand, when you check the
weather just before departure you find that the forecast
has been amended to include an occasional ceiling of
1,000 feet overcast and 1 mile visibility for the period
between one hour before scheduled arrival to one hour
after, you must file an alternate before you take off.

Under the first scenario, if you check the
weather while airborne when you have less than an hour
until landing and find that Lexington is reporting
weather that is still below 2,000 and 3, must you file
an alternate? No. Again, filing an alternate is strictly
a flight planning exercise. But you are expected to use
good judgment in the conduct of the flight. That means
that you know you have some place to go and more
than enough fuel to get there.

If you arrive at Lexington and cannot land because the airport is below landing minimums you can
hold for a while to see if conditions improve. An air-

craft operated under Part 91 of the FARs can fly the approach and land if the criteria in FAR 91.175 are met (See Appendix B). So, the question is how many times will you try the approach and how long will you loiter in the area burning up fuel?

If you are on top of things you will check the weather just before arriving in the Lexington area. Considering that you may need a place to go, you find that Cincinnati's Lunken Field is above ILS landing minimums and expected to stay that way. You plan on going there if you cannot land at Lexington. The flying time is about 30 minutes plus another five to 10 minutes for an approach. How much fuel will you want in the tanks as a minimum when leaving Lexington for Cincinnati?

If you consider that normal alternate planning considerations require 45 minutes of fuel remaining after arrival at the legal alternate, that is a good place to start in our hypothetical situation. You cannot plan to leave Lexington with only 40 minutes of fuel or your engine might go silent on final approach, especially if you are delayed due to traffic or some other unforeseen event. Good judgment is the difference between having plenty of fuel in the tanks when you land at Cincinnati or never getting there because you run them dry before you arrive.

I remember reading about a Boeing 747 flying from Europe to Kennedy International Airport in New York City years ago. The weather in New York was poor and no one was landing. The 747 held for some time before the crew decided to go to the flight plan alternate, Newark, New Jersey (EWK). As the airplane touched down at Newark three of the airplane's

254 Flying On The Gages

four engines failed because of fuel starvation. That was cutting it a little too close.

While looking into the incident the FAA discovered that the airline involved routinely figured its alternate fuel requirements using a straight-line distance between the destination airport and the alternate airport. In the New York area there is no such thing as a straight line between airports when the weather is IFR. In fact, the flight from JFK to EWK required nearly 30 minutes when the airline figured it would only take 10.

The 747 pilots used bad judgment in that incident because they did not allow for enough remaining fuel at their alternate landing site. They held too long over JFK before deciding to go to Newark, and probably did not realize that the flight to the alternate would take as long as it did. There are several lessons to be learned from this mishap.

Keep in mind that you probably won't get direct routing to your alternate.

If you decide to hold at Lexington keep an eye on the Cincinnati weather. If it appears that it is deteriorating you must get there before it goes below minimums or find another airport that you have sufficient fuel reserve to reach. And keep in mind that you probably will not get direct routing from one airport to the other. Never plan to land with less than 45 minutes of fuel remaining, no matter what airport you use for an alternate. That means you must leave the Lexington area for Cincinnati when you have 1 hour and 25 minutes of fuel left in the tanks.

How do you know exactly how much fuel is left? Don't rely on fuel gages to tell you. The gages in most light airplanes are unreliable. You must know how many gallons your airplane's engine(s) burns per hour and keep track of the flight time. That is the most reliable method of knowing what is left in the tanks.

Up to now we have been discussing when you must file an alternate with your IFR flight plan, but you also need to know what qualifies an airport to be a legal alternate. To begin with there are standard alternate minimums. For an airport that has a precision approach available for use the forecast must indicate a ceiling of at least 600 feet and a visibility of 2 miles at the time you would arrive at the alternate. An airport that has a non-precision approach available for use must have a forecast ceiling of at least 800 feet and a visibility of at least 2 miles at the time of arrival.

Special circumstances like high terrain nearby or unusual prevailing weather phenomena may dictate that higher minimums must be used at some airports. Before designating an airport as an alternate, look at its page in the Jeppesen approach plates for any other-than-standard minimums that may apply. In the NOS plates they are listed in the front of each book of plates under "Alternate Minimums."

For example, you are planning a flight into Indianapolis, Indiana and the weather dictates that you find a suitable alternate. After checking the chart you decide that Bloomington, Indiana will work. It is 37 miles from Indianapolis and has an ILS approach, and although a forecast is not issued for Bloomington, the area forecast indicates that the weather will be above the 600 and 2 standard required for a precision approach.

Before you list Bloomington as the alternate you need to do some homework. Is it an acceptable alternate? Take out your Jepps and look on the airport page of the Bloomington approach plates. In the lower right corner you will find a box with the alternate information. The first thing to note is that Bloomington is not available as an alternate when the control tower is closed, because there would be no one there to issue weather reports. You will want to check on the tower's hours of operation to make sure that it will be open when you need to use it as an alternate.

Otherwise the alternate minimums are standard for precision and non-precision approaches except that if the VOR or GPS approaches to Runway 6 or 24 are in use the aircraft must be equipped with DME. Also, the localizer approach and NDB approach to Runway 35 are not authorized for alternate minimums. So, the ILS or VOR/DME must be in service if an approach to Runway 35 is considered as an alternate. The same information can be found in the Indiana/Ohio book of the NOS approach plates (see Figure 1) in the IFR Alternate Minimums section.

You cannot select an airport for an alternate without checking if it has other than standard minimums.

Now you know that you cannot select an airport for an alternate without checking to see if it has other than standard minimums or restrictions as to which approaches can be considered. When using Bloomington for an alternate you need to look at the weather and wind conditions to determine which approaches qualify. For example, if the wind was out of the south at 20 gusting to 30 you could not count on the ILS to Runway 35 for your approach. You could select the VOR approach to Runway 17, but then the area forecasts would have to indicate that the ceiling and visibility would be at least 800 and 2 when you will arrive. The ILS to Runway 35 is the only approach at Bloomington that can allow you to use the airport as an alternate when the weather is forecast to be as low as 600 and 2.

BLOOMINGTON, IN
MONROE COUNTY .... ILS Rwy 35¹
VOR/DME Rwy 35²
VOR or GPS Rwy 6³
VOR or GPS Rwy 17²#
VOR or GPS Rwy 24³
¹ILS, NA when control tower closed. LOC, NA.
²NA when contol tower closed.
³NA when control tower closed; NA for
non-DME aircraft.
#Category D, 800-2¼.

Figure 1

I always attempt to list an alternate that I intend to use if I cannot land at my original destination. For example, if I am flying into Pontiac, Michigan and an alternate is required I usually select Flint. It is reasonably close to Pontiac, has two ILS approaches, weather reporting, and a terminal forecast. While enroute I keep abreast of the weather at Flint and Pontiac, and if Flint appears to be going below alternate minimums I look for another airport that I can count on in case I cannot land at either Pontiac or Flint.

But there are times when none of the local airports meet the alternate minimum requirements. For example, if Flint's forecast is calling for 1,000 broken and 2 miles with an occasional 400 overcast and 1, I cannot use it for a legal alternate. But if I didn't get into Pontiac I would fly the ILS at Flint if the airport was reporting weather above landing minimums, though my legal alternate might be somewhere else, say Fort Wayne, Indiana. You are not required to fly to your legal alternate if you don't get into your intended destination. This is where good judgment is required.

I recommend that whenever possible you should land with enough fuel in your tanks to get to your legal alternate plus a 45 minute reserve. That is the preflight planning requirement, and it makes sense for pilots to live with it during the flight.

For example, you fly the ILS approach to Pontiac and don't get in. Your alternate is Fort Wayne but Flint is reporting weather above landing minimums at 300 overcast and 2 miles. By attempting to get into Flint you are using your reserve fuel, and if you make a successful landing nothing is lost. But how many approaches would you make at Flint before deciding you were not going to get in there either? And if you could not get in there where would you go next? If you maintain enough fuel on board to get to your alternate plus the 45 minute reserve you should always have a place to go.

But some pilots, because they refuse to stop for fuel along the way, make their airplanes "fuel critical" from the moment they take off. Their flight planning is so close that the numbers barely work, and the slightest change in the winds aloft sees them eating into their reserve fuel. When they get near their destination they are already low on fuel, and often they don't have enough left to go to an alternate, even a close-in one. So, if the weather goes down the tubes at the original destination they are in serious trouble because they failed to leave themselves a way out.

Fuel is like money in the bank.
You can never have too much of it.

Fuel is like money in the bank. You can never have too much of it. Light singles and some twins don't offer much IFR range because of the legal requirements for alternate fuel. For example, my Piper Arrow has 48 gallons of useable fuel and burns 10 gallons per hour on a trip, giving it a fuel range of 4.8 hours. A couple of times a year my wife and I fly to the east coast from our home base near Pontiac, Michigan. The distance to the airport at Lincoln, Rhode Island is 557 nautical miles and my flight planning computer says it will take four hours and 15 minutes non-stop in a straight line between the two points. That leaves 33 minutes of fuel left in the tanks on arrival.

I cannot plan to fly non-stop on an IFR flight plan unless the weather is forecast to be above that required for filing an alternate. But I never allow my fuel supply to get that low, no matter what kind of airplane I am flying or the purpose for the flight. So, I stop for fuel along the way, usually at Utica, New York.

The flight to Utica takes just under three hours including the time for an approach and, though it is all on airways, the route is nearly straight line. That leaves me an hour and 48 minutes of fuel left in the tanks upon landing. The second leg to Lincoln takes an hour and 35 minutes including time for an approach, so I have plenty of fuel in reserve in case the weather does not do what I expect. The last two trips we made have been in instrument weather with approaches at both airports.

Making the fuel stop at Utica lets me loiter over my destination airport if it is below landing minimums and I feel the weather will improve. Though it is doubtful that I would hold for very long, I could stay in a holding pattern for some time before I got to the point where I was left with the amount of fuel necessary to fly to my alternate plus 45 minutes. Of course the location of my alternate could be close-in or some distance away depending on how bad the weather was.

Having that much fuel at my destination gives me plenty of options. I could fly to another airport and try several approaches in marginal conditions and still have the fuel to get to my alternate and beyond. And I am reassured to know there is plenty of fuel in the tanks, instead of squirming in my seat wondering when the engine is going to quit because the gages are hovering on the empty marks.

When you do your flight planning you must consider local conditions that can cause problems. For example, Lincoln is close to Narragansett Bay and is subject to fog when the winds are out of the south. If I had a tail wind heading east it would be tempting to skip the stop at Utica, but I know how fast fog moves up the bay and the peculiarities of the ATC system in the Northeast. I would not want to be caught without plenty of fuel in the tanks and somewhere to go.

Too many pilots don't take the time to do good flight planning. That is what eventually gets them into trouble. If they sat down with a chart, worked the numbers, and saw how tight their proposed trip was, they would stop for fuel instead of pushing so hard that their engine(s) run dry on approach.

CHAPTER NINETEEN

THE MISSED APPROACH

The other day a friend told me that she was close to going for her instrument checkride, but one problem was still plaguing her. She was busting minimums before starting the missed approach procedure on an ILS approach. From the description of her last dual flight it was easy to see that she was having the same problem that many instrument pilots face when they fly a missed approach procedure from an ILS.

Most instrument flight instructors teach their students to fly the ILS right down to decision height before looking for the runway. In the training environment they want the approach flown to minimums be-

cause any time the student looks up he or she should
see the runway directly in front of the airplane if the
procedure is flown correctly while using a view-limit-
ing device. But it is different in the real world of flying low approaches. Essentially, you fly the airplane
to DH, but you must prepare yourself for the go-around
before reaching minimums if you are to keep the airplane at or above DH while deciding whether to land
or miss the approach.

Too many pilots don't even look at the missed
approach procedure before beginning an approach because they are sure, from the weather report, that it
will not be necessary. If the ATIS is advertising 1,000
overcast and 2 miles there is little doubt in the minds
of most pilots that they will make a successful approach.
But that assumption is mistaken. Many times over the
years I have heard a weather report like that on the
ATIS but found the real weather to be much lower, in
some cases at or below minimums. ATC may direct
you to miss the approach because of problems on the
runway or a perceived traffic conflict. If no other instructions are given to you the controller expects you
to fly the published missed approach. If you don't know
what that is, at least the first element of it, your go-
around will be delayed.

*The missed approach procedure
begins long before the aircraft
gets to DH or MDA.*

The missed approach procedure begins long before the aircraft gets to DH or MDA. Its true beginning is when you brief yourself on the approach you

are going to fly, because that is when you must look it over so you understand what is required should you need to go around.

There is no such thing as a standard missed approach procedure because the environment around each airport is different. Terrain features, manmade obstructions, and communications and navaid reception all dictate how each instrument approach must be flown as well as the associated missed approach procedure.

Some new or barely current instrument pilots give little thought to the missed approach procedure because they are busy enough trying to keep the airplane on the course prescribed by the approach plate or ATC. These pilots are behind the airplane instead of maintaining a mental position ahead of it, and as they study the approach plate their heading or altitude wanders. As they look back at their instruments they discover their dilemma and quickly try to correct for it. Meanwhile, the localizer or VOR radial starts its trek to the center of the display and all thoughts of looking back at the approach plate are forgotten with the new urgency to fly the approach. An instructor on board who asks his charge about the missed approach at that point will probably be ignored because the pilot has no time to go back and refresh himself or herself on the procedure while trying to keep the airplane on the approach course.

Pilots must recognize that a missed approach procedure is part of the actual approach and must be treated as such. It cannot be ignored because the pilot does not get to it for whatever reason. Those who don't consider the missed approach because they are too busy flying the airplane need more instruction. They are

not far enough ahead of the airplane they are flying
and could get into serious trouble if the slightest thing
goes wrong.

More experienced pilots tend to disregard the
missed approach procedure if the weather is above landing minimums. The trouble with that, as I stated earlier, is that what is advertised on the ATIS or AWOS is
not always what they see when they get down to DH or
MDA. If they hear that others are landing out of the
approach they figure the missed approach will not be
necessary, but when they get to DH and cannot locate
the runway environment they are faced with figuring
out the missed approach procedure. That means reading the approach plate while keeping the airplane level
during flight very close to the ground. We have noted
in earlier chapters that any time a pilot's attention is
diverted from flying the airplane an accident can result. The closer an aircraft is to the ground the higher
the pilot's situational awareness must be, but the reality is often the reverse.

Missed approaches, like instrument approaches,
may be very simple or extremely complicated. The
more complicated the procedure, the higher the awareness level of the pilot needs to be. He or she must
understand the go-around and carry it out to the letter
to ensure that the aircraft is never in jeopardy because
it gets too close to high terrain or other obstacles. But
before we look at any actual missed approach procedures let's go back to my friend's problem with busting minimums, since that is one step before the go-
around begins, should it be necessary.

One of her concerns was that she flew to DH
and looked up for the runway, the instructor told her

to go around as if she did not see it, and she made the missed approach. Then, as she began the go-around procedure her instructor informed her that had that approach been part of a checkride, she would have flunked because she busted minimums. Apparently this has happened several times.

The airplane should never be flown
level at DH while the pilot searches
for the runway.

The pilot must be the master of his or her airplane and be thinking far ahead of it at all times, but especially at this point. If there is no indication of breaking out of the clouds prior to 100 feet above DH the pilot must start thinking about making the missed approach that he or she briefed on earlier. The airplane is flown down to DH but under no circumstances is it to go below that altitude without the required visibility and runway environment in sight. The airplane should never be flown level at DH while the pilot continues his or her search for the runway. The choices are: (1) the runway is in sight and the final phase of the landing is completed, or (2) it is not and the missed approach sequence starts.

My friend's problem, which afflicts many others as well, is that she is not mentally prepared to begin the missed approach at DH. Her mind is still focused on the approach itself because she considers the missed approach to be a separate procedure. Complicating the issue is that her instructor insists that she cannot look out the window until reaching DH. In the real world it does not work that way.

If the missed approach is to be started before the airplane goes below DH the pilot must look out the window between 25 and 50 feet before reaching the bottom of the approach. This is the tough part because if the airplane is still in the clouds and there are no visual cues the pilot's eyes are split between flying the instruments and looking for the runway environment. But if the search for the runway is not begun slightly above DH, the pilot has to either level out or go below minimums when the magic altitude is attained. If the pilot looks just before DH he or she can initiate the go-around immediately on reaching it.

Avoid looking back and forth
repeatedly between the instruments
and the view outside.

The pilot who is ahead of his or her airplane will use peripheral vision during the descent on the glide slope to determine whether the airplane is still in the clouds, although caution must be taken to avoid being fooled. If there is a defined cloud base at 600 feet above DH there could be another layer below. But if you are certain that you are out of the clouds you could peek out the window to see if the runway is in sight. But don't remove your eyes from the panel for any longer than necessary, and avoid looking back and forth repeatedly between the instruments and the view outside the window. If you believe that you are in clouds stay on the gages until reaching that point between 25 and 50 feet above DH where you begin your search for the runway environment.

Non-precision approaches are different because

there is no vertical guidance from the ground. At the final fix the pilot begins the descent to the minimum descent altitude (MDA) where he or she levels off and then searches for the airport and runway. Minimums for these approaches are higher than those for precision approaches, but still the pilot must not fly beyond the missed approach point at MDA unless the runway is in sight with the required visibility or the airplane is beginning the missed approach procedure.

Our discussion thus far has centered on getting to the missed approach point but our primary purpose for conducting any instrument approach is to make a landing out of it. No matter if a landing or missed approach results, the airplane must be positioned properly at DH or MDA so either the runway can be located or the missed approach procedure can begin from its intended starting point. That is very important, especially when there is terrain or some other obstacle confronting the aircraft.

If the pilot levels the airplane off at DH and continues to fly straight ahead or fly beyond the missed approach point on a non-precision approach, he or she might compromise the aircraft's safety when the missed approach is finally begun. If there is rising terrain on the other side of the airport the missed approach procedure is designed to keep the aircraft clear of it, but only if it is begun at the designated point along the approach. All climb and turning considerations are based on the distance from the terrain at the missed approach point.

Now on to the missed approach itself. First we will start with one that is not too complicated. This type is usually found at the end of an approach where the ground radio station used for the approach is right on the airport. For example, the missed approach for the VOR Runway 27 approach at Gaylord, Michigan (see Figure 1) is about as simple as they come.

The VOR is on the airport and it is the missed approach point. The airplane passes the VOR and begins a climbing right turn to 3,000 feet while entering the depicted holding pattern. The navigation radio is already set up for the missed approach because the inbound radial in the hold is the same as the final approach course.

There is no reason not to begin the missed approach procedure at the VOR because if you have not spotted the runway by then you probably are not going to see it. And even if you did locate it at the VOR, you would be too high to make a straight-in landing approach on it because the VOR is at least halfway down the runway. You could circle to land if you were at or above circling minimums and your view of the airport was sufficient to allow a safe approach, but if you didn't locate the runway until you were directly over the airport it is doubtful that you'll have the required visibility to circle back to the runway.

The missed approach for the Runway 28 VOR or GPS approach into Owosso, Michigan (see Figure 2) is more complicated, but not because there is rising terrain. You will notice that the 278-degree radial of the Flint VOR is used for the approach and that it is 17.4 miles from the station to the airport. Whoever designed this approach decided to use crossing radials off the Flint VOR and the Saginaw (MBS) VOR to form the OWOSO intersection and position the missed approach holding pattern there. The holding pattern is

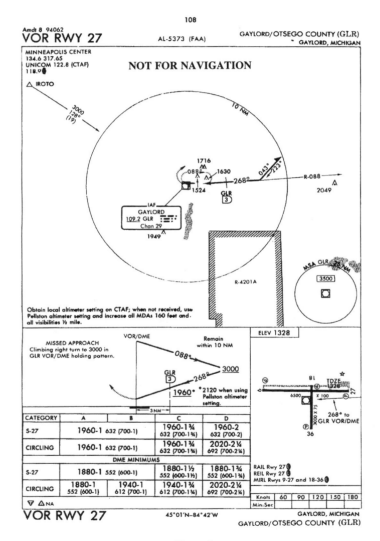

108

Amdt 8 94062
VOR RWY 27   AL-5373 (FAA)   GAYLORD/OTSEGO COUNTY (GLR)
GAYLORD, MICHIGAN

MINNEAPOLIS CENTER
134.6 317.65
UNICOM 122.8 (CTAF)
118.9

NOT FOR NAVIGATION

Figure 1

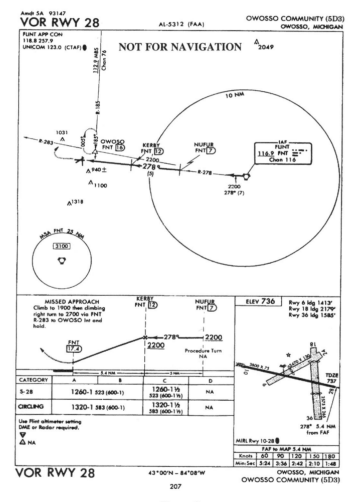

Amdt 5A 93147

VOR RWY 28   AL-5312 (FAA)   OWOSSO COMMUNITY (5D3)
                                                OWOSSO, MICHIGAN

FLINT APP CON
118.8 257.9
UNICOM 123.0 (CTAF) ●   **NOT FOR NAVIGATION**   △2049

Figure 2

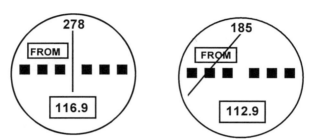

Figure 3A
At The Missed Approach Point Of The VOR RWY 28 Approach

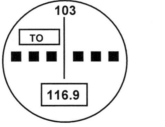
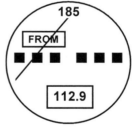

Figure 3B
Upon Intercepting The Flint 283° Radial Inbound To OWOSO Intersection

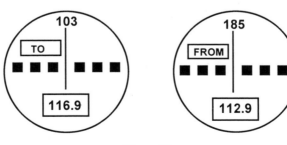

Figure 3C
At The OWOSO Intersection

perpendicular to the approach and the pilot must be certain to follow the missed approach instructions carefully or face the possibility of flying past the OWOSO intersection without realizing it. The procedure calls for the pilot to climb to 1,900 feet, then begin a climbing right turn to 2,700 feet to intercept the Flint 283-degree radial inbound to the OWOSO intersection (see Figure 3). Several instructors have informed me that they use this procedure for training because pilots don't realize how close they are to the intersection when the missed approach procedure is begun and often fly past it, continuing toward the Flint VOR. Another reason for missing the intersection is because the students do not understand how the VOR works and set up the Flint VOR wrong, usually so it is reverse-sensing. Then, though the number two nav is properly set to the Saginaw 185-degree radial, they don't understand what the needle deflections before and after the OWOSO intersection should look like. So unless they see the needle center as they cross the designated radial they don't know where they are in relation to the intersection. And should they see the Saginaw 185-degree radial center before they intercept the Flint 283 they become confused.

The FAA doesn't care how you enter the hold as long as you remain within the designated airspace.

Another problem with this procedure is how to enter the hold. My preference is to always remain within the holding airspace, so I would make a sharp left turn to approximately 330 degrees, depending on the wind, and do a teardrop entry. But this is more difficult than a parallel entry, which would likely be the choice of most pilots. Remember, the FAA does not care how you enter a holding pattern as long as you remain within airspace designated for the procedure.

The wind should have a direct bearing on how the entry is performed. That is because a strong westerly wind will push the aircraft toward the Flint VOR and a turn into the pattern for the teardrop entry, while decreasing the ground speed considerably, would prevent the aircraft from being blown too far away. But a parallel entry that is not adjusted properly for the wind will mean a struggle to get back to the OWOSO intersection to enter the hold. If the pilot has no knowledge of the winds at 3,000 feet he or she could be blown out of the protected airspace while on the northbound leg of the outside parallel entry, find it extremely difficult to get aligned on the Saginaw 185-degree radial, or both.

Before accepting any approach be certain that if you miss, you have the onboard capability to comply with the missed approach procedure. For example, some airplanes don't have ADF capability yet the missed approach procedure for an ILS or VOR approach clearly calls for it. You cannot begin the approach, no matter what the weather is, if you don't have the equipment required to complete the missed approach procedure. That is another reason for an early review of the approach plates and missed approach procedures at your destination airport.

CHAPTER TWENTY

HOLDING PATTERNS

The last time I did a complete turn in a holding pattern was about three years ago. I was bound for State College, Pennsylvania in a Cessna 421 with a plane loaded with passengers eager to see the Michigan-Penn State football game. We were already late because of low ceilings and reduced visibility in fog between Ann Arbor and State College. Our destination weather was very slow to improve so there were several airplanes waiting for their chance at the ILS approach to Runway 24.

Considering the weather and the lack of radar

at State College I was not surprised when I was issued the holding instructions. "One seven five Alpha Mike, after Phillipsburg fly direct to the Penue Outer Compass Locator and hold as published. Maintain 6,000."

I had the approach plate in front of me and was pleased to discover that my favorite entry, the teardrop, would work fine for this pattern entry. The winds were very light on the surface and at altitude, so there was nothing difficult in this procedure. I flew the pattern twice before getting my clearance for the approach. Though my passengers missed their tailgate party they made it to the game just as the opening kickoff was flying through the air.

Nobody likes holding patterns. For aircraft owners and operators they are costly and not a very efficient use of resources. Neither pilots nor passengers like to fly in circles directly over their destination. And when planes are stacked up one on top of the other controllers get nervous because they have a large number of IFR airplanes in a small block of airspace. Fortunately we don't have to hold often because our ATC system is far superior to any other with radar coverage that allows one aircraft to follow another on approaches across most of our country.

We don't do enough holding patterns to stay proficient at them.

From a pilot's perspective there are two problems with holding patterns. First, we don't do enough of them to stay proficient at them, and second, the fact that we are seldom obliged to hold leads to a definite lack of enthusiasm for practicing them.

Missed approach procedures almost always lead to holding patterns, but due to the caliber of our ATC system we hardly ever get that far in a missed approach procedure. We look at the plate before beginning an approach so we know what is required of us, but most of the time if we don't spot the airport or runway we are looking for, when we switch back to the radar controller he or she has us re-identified and gives us vectors for another shot at the same approach, or to another airport of our choosing.

Flying a good holding pattern requires practice because the wind at the holding altitude does its best to see that our intended racetrack pattern looks more like an oblong or a circle. If we were able to watch our performance on a controller's radar screen, I imagine many holding patterns would look like a blob.

No matter what it looks like, though, the important thing is that we stay within our allotted holding airspace so there are no conflicts with other airplanes. And if you happen to be holding using an ADF, the potential for error doubles. Few people use ADFs for serious navigation in this country any more. Most pilots lack the proficiency to fly a decent holding pattern using one.

That instrument pilots understand the concept of holding patterns, there is little doubt. A racetrack pattern is a racetrack pattern. It's easy to visualize what it looks like when on the ground, but when the controller says those awful words, "Proceed to the ABC fix and hold north, one minute legs, left turns," it is like being sapped on the back of the head by the Louisville Slugger that any sane flight instructor keeps under the seat to deal with obstinate instrument students.

Like everything else we do in aviation, holding patterns in themselves are not that difficult. But in the context of an entire flight, along with everything else required of the pilot, why they are scorned becomes more apparent.

Most holding patterns we are required to fly are associated with an arrival airport. Usually we are at the end of a flight and chances are that fatigue is working its way into the cockpit at the same time. The weather is undoubtedly poor or we would have no reason to hold, and that means we are staring at a low approach once we reach the bottom of the holding stack.

After the holding clearance is read back the first thing the pilot needs to do is locate the holding fix, if he or she is not already familiar with it. Then it's necessary to figure the holding direction in relation to the fix and determine the best method for entering the pattern.

The easiest way to enter any hold is via the direct entry.

The easiest way to enter any hold is via the direct entry. If you were flying east along V103 east of the Lansing (LAN) VOR (see Figure 1) and received a clearance to hold west of the SPRTN intersection on V103, you would enter the published hold on a direct entry. When you reach SPRTN you are established in the hold because you are in a position to begin the pattern from that point. By the time you reach SPRTN you should have a good handle on the winds and know what to expect in the pattern if your cruising altitude is the same as the holding altitude you are assigned.

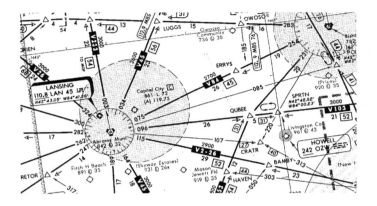

Figure 1

If you were cleared to SPRTN from the northeast along the Flint 220-degree radial, a parallel entry would be appropriate. As you cross SPRTN you would fly a heading that would parallel the holding course. Since the inbound heading is 96 degrees the parallel heading would be 276 degrees. After one minute you would make a right turn back to the fix, after which you would fly the pattern.

If you departed the Howell Airport with a clearance direct to SPRTN to hold as published, you would cross SPRTN intersection on your northbound heading to begin the teardrop entry. Then you would turn left 30 degrees, fly outbound for one minute, followed by a left turn back to the fix. You would then be established in the pattern and fly it as published.

The legs on holding patterns are all one minute unless ATC approves something else. For example, in most high density areas pilots ask for either five or 10 mile legs. Once, when flying through the Pittsburgh area, I heard a controller issuing 20 mile legs to aircraft assigned to hold without being asked. It is much easier to keep track of mileage on the DME than watching the sweep second hand on a clock, or resetting a digital timer every time you reach the one minute limit. ATC will normally allow the mileage legs as long as there is no conflicting traffic at your holding altitude.

One reason that holding patterns earn the animosity of pilots is because it is difficult to figure out which entry is best. While all the instrument flight manuals tout the three entries I briefly described above, the truth is that you can enter a holding pattern any way you want as long as you don't bust your holding airspace. I prefer to use the teardrop entry whenever possible because it keeps me inside the pattern itself. As long as I stay inside the pattern I know I am in protected airspace. Sometimes it takes a long initial turn at the fix to make a teardrop entry, but if a pilot's positional awareness is high, and he or she is familiar with what the winds are doing at the assigned altitude, it can be done with only slightly more difficulty than flying a parallel entry.

If I were coming down the Flint 220-degree radial on reaching SPRTN I would make a right turn to 310 degrees (assumng no wind), fly that heading for one minute, then turn left back to the fix to begin the hold. If I had a wind from the west I would cut the turn short at 290 degrees, fly that heading for a minute and 10 seconds or so, depending on the wind velocity, then turn back to the fix. If the wind was strong out of the east I would fly the parallel entry instead of taking a chance on being blown out of the holding airspace, which could happen easily between the long turn outbound and the outbound leg.

So, how do you decide how you will enter a particular hold? Some pilots buy a plastic device, which depicts the three types of entries, and lay it top of the holding fix. Then, depending on which direction they approach the fix from, they pick out the appropriate entry. Others draw lines on their charts depicting their heading and the holding pattern, if it is not shown, in an attempt to decide which is the best method of entry. Another method is to visualize the holding pattern on your direction indicator, which basically works like drawing lines on the chart.

You can enter the hold any way you see fit as long as you don't bust the holding airspace.

Unless you are based at an airport that has no radar coverage and you expect to fly in there on instruments regularly you will seldom need to fly a holding pattern. That doesn't excuse you from having a plan to enter the hold should you be given one. So, what should you do? If you are an instrument student your instructor will insist that you use one of the three entry methods, and you will likely be called on by the designated examiner to demonstrate one of them during your checkride. But in reality you can enter the hold any way you see fit as long as you don't bust the holding airspace.

An aerobatic entry probably would not be suitable, but if you use your head and understand what the winds are doing to you it should not be too difficult to turn inside the pattern, or just outside of it, with a secondary turn back to the fix from which the holding pattern begins. Positional and situational awareness are important. When you receive the holding clearance use one of the three entry methods or develop a plan for entering the hold so by the time you cross the fix you know exactly what you want to do and how you want to do it.

One problem many pilots have with holding entries is that they stare at their chart for a long time and never decide about the entry. Then, when they cross the fix they are still lost. Now that they have to do something they still don't have the foggiest idea of what it should be. Doing anything in an airplane out of ignorance or sheer frustration is asking for trouble.

If the holding pattern is not depicted on the chart or instrument approach plate it is much harder to visualize an entry, which creates the many problems. If the controller told you to hold west of the QUBEE intersection (see Figure 1) using left turns, there is nothing difficult about that one because the SPRTN intersection hold is depicted east of Qubee with left turns. Be certain that you don't mix the two up and fly beyond QUBEE to SPRTN thinking that is where you are to hold.

If the controller told you to hold east of QUBEE, left turns, could you handle that one? Remember, on the inbound leg you always fly toward the fix with a left turn away from it when you cross. That means that the pattern east of QUBEE would be flown south of V103 except for the inbound leg that would be on the airway. Some pilots reverse that and fly the inbound leg north of V103 with a left turn into the fix, followed by the outbound leg on the airway. That is not the correct way to fly a holding pattern.

Don't accept a holding clearance without an EFC.

When you are assigned a holding pattern you should be issued an "expect-further-clearance time," or EFC. This is extremely important because should you lose communications with ATC after you are established in the hold the controller will expect you to leave the hold at the EFC. Don't accept a holding clearance without an EFC.

What speed do you fly your aircraft in a hold? Reducing speed makes the pattern much easier to fly and reduces your fuel consumption. That's especially critical in jets that are holding at low altitudes. But don't carry it too far. Find a comfortable speed to fly the pattern that works for your airplane. It should not be so slow that you are flying around with the stall horn buzzing in your ear, nor do you want to pull the power back so far that the cylinder head temperature is out of its normal operating range.

One more thing about holding patterns. Don't turn the radio down while you are in the hold because you want to talk to one of your passengers. Most of the times I have had to hold I was re-cleared out of the holding pattern before my EFC. If you sit back thinking you will not hear from ATC until your EFC you could tie up much of the airspace when you fail to respond to a call to descend or proceed out of the hold.

Holding patterns give pilots fits only because they are seldom used. They are likely to be with us for a long time, though, and it behooves every instrument pilot to be prepared to execute one whenever necessary. Besides weather related delays there could be problems on the airport you intend to land at that stop all traffic for some time. I remember having to hold to get into LaGuardia Airport when the weather was VFR and I could see the airport from 6,000 feet, though it is highly unlikely that most of us flying into general aviation airports would experience that kind of delay. So, as much as you may detest holding patterns be sure you are prepared for them if you hear the words, "Hold east, left turns, one minute legs."

APPENDIX A

FAR 91.169

**91.169 IFR FLIGHT PLAN: INFORMATION RE-
QUIRED**

(a) Information required. Unless otherwise authorized by ATC. each person filing an IFR flight plan
shall include in it the following information:

(1) Information required under 91.153(a).

(2) An alternate airport, except as provided in
paragraph (b) of this section.

(b) Exceptions to applicability of paragraph
(a)(2) of this section. Paragraph (a)(2) of this section
does not apply if Part 97 of this chapter prescribes a

standard instrument approach procedure for the first airport of intended landing and. for at least I hour before and I hour after the estimated time of arrival, the weather reports or forecasts, or any combination of them, indicate-

(1) The ceiling will be at least 2,000 feet above the airport elevation; and

(2) The visibility will be at least 3 statute miles.

(c) IFR alternate airport weather minimums. Unless otherwise authorized by the Administrator, no person may include an alternate airport in an IFR flight plan unless current weather forecasts indicate that, at the estimated time of arrival at the alternate airport, the ceiling and visibility at that airport will be at or above the following alternate airport weather minimums:

(1) If an instrument approach procedure has been published in Part 97 of this chapter for that airport, the alternate airport minimums specified in that procedure or, if none are so specified, the following minimums:

(i) Precision approach procedure: Ceiling 600 feet and visibility 2 statute miles.

(ii) Nonprecision approach procedure: Ceiling 800 feet and visibility 2 statute miles.

(2) If no instrument approach procedure has been published in Part 97 of this chapter for that airport, the ceiling and visibility minimums are those allowing descent from the MEA, approach, and landing under basic VFR.

(d) Cancellation. When a flight plan has been activated, the pilot in command, upon canceling   or completing the flight under the flight plan, shall notify an FAA Flight Service Station or ATC facility.

APPENDIX B

91.175 TAKEOFF AND LANDING UNDER IFR

(a) Instrument approaches to civil airports. Unless otherwise authorized by the Administrator, when an instrument letdown to a civil airport is necessary, each person operating an aircraft, except a military aircraft of the United States, shall use a standard instrument approach procedure prescribed for the airport in Part 97 of this chapter.

(b) Authorized DH or MDA. For the purpose of this section, when the approach procedure being used provides for and requires the use of a DH or MDA, the authorized DH or MDA is the highest of the following:

(1) The DH or MDA prescribed by the approach procedure.

(2) The DH or MDA prescribed for the pilot in command.

(3) The DH or MDA for which the aircraft is equipped.

(c) Operation below DH or MDA. Where a DH or MDA is applicable, no pilot may operate an aircraft, except a military aircraft of the United States, at any airport below the authorized MDA or continue an approach below the authorized DH unless-

(1)The aircraft is continuously in a position from which a descent to a landing on the intended   runway can be made at a normal rate of descent using normal maneuvers, and for operations conducted under Part 121 or Part 135 unless that descent rate will allow touchdown to occur within the touchdown zone of the runway of intended landing;

(2)The flight visibility is not less than the visibility prescribed in the standard instrument approach being used; and

(3)Except for a Category II or Category III approach where any necessary visual reference requirements are specified by the Administrator, at least one of the following visual references for the intended runway is distinctly visible and identifiable to the pilot:

(i)The approach light system, except that the pilot may not descend below 100 feet above the touchdown zone elevation using the approach lights as a reference unless the red terminating bars or the red side row bars are also distinctly visible and identifiable.

(ii)   The threshold.
(iii)   The threshold markings.
(iv)   The threshold lights.
(v)   The runway end identifier lights.
(vi)   The visual approach slope indicator.
(vii)   The touchdown zone or touchdown zone markings.
(viii) The touchdown zone lights.
(ix)   The runway or runway markings.
(x)   The runway lights.

(d) Landing. No pilot operating an aircraft, except a military aircraft of the United States, may land that aircraft when the flight visibility is less than the visibility prescribed in the standard instrument approach procedure being used.

(e) Missed approach procedures. Each pilot operating an aircraft, except a military aircraft of the United States, shall immediately execute an appropriate missed approach procedure when either of the following conditions exist:

(1) Whenever the requirements of paragraph (c) of this section are not met at either of the following times:

(i) When the aircraft is being operated below MDA; or

(ii) Upon arrival at the missed approach point, including a DH where a DH is specified and its use is required, and at any time after that until touchdown.

(2) Whenever an identifiable part of the airport is not distinctly visible to the pilot during a circling maneuver at or above MDA, unless the inability to see

an identifiable part of the airport results only from a normal bank of the aircraft during the circling approach.

(f) Civil airport takeoff minimums. Unless otherwise authorized by the Administrator, no pilot operating an aircraft under Parts 121, 125, 127, 129, or 135 of this chapter may take off from a civil airport under IFR unless weather conditions are at or above the weather minimums for IFR takeoff prescribed for that airport under Part 97 of this chapter. If takeoff minimums are not prescribed   under Part 97 of this chapter for a particular airport, the following minimums apply to takeoffs under IFR for aircraft operating under those Parts:

(1) For aircraft, other than helicopters, having two engines or less-1 statute mile visibility.

(2) For aircraft having more than two engines-1/2 statute mile visibility.

(3) For helicopters-1/2 statute mile visibility.

(g) Military airports. Unless otherwise prescribed by the Administrator, each person operating a civil aircraft under IFR into or out of a military airport shall comply with the instrument approach procedures and the takeoff and landing minimum prescribed by the military authority having   jurisdiction of that airport.

(h) Comparable values of RVR and ground visibility.

(1) Except for Category II or Category III minimums, if RVR minimums for takeoff or landing are prescribed in an instrument approach procedure, but RVR is not reported for the runway of intended opera-

tion, the RVR minimum shall be converted to ground visibility in accordance with the table in paragraph (h)(2) of this section and shall be the visibility minimum for takeoff or landing on that runway.

(2)RVR Table:
RVR (feet) visibility (statute miles)

........................1,600 1/4
........................2,400 1/2
........................3,200 5/8
........................4,000 3/4
........................4,500 7/8
........................8,000   1

(i) Operations on unpublished routes and use of radar in instrument approach procedures. When radar is approved at certain locations for ATC purposes, it may be used not only for surveillance and precision radar approaches, as applicable, but also may be used in conjunction with instrument approach procedures predicated on other types of radio navigational aids. Radar vectors may be   authorized to provide course guidance through the segments of an approach to the final course or fix. When operating on an unpublished route or while being radar vectored, the pilot, when an approach clearance is received, shall, in addition to complying with 91.177, maintain the last altitude assigned to that pilot until the aircraft is established on a segment of a published route or instrument approach procedure unless a different altitude is assigned by ATC. After the aircraft is so established, published altitudes apply to descent within each succeeding route or approach segment unless a different altitude is assigned by ATC. Upon reaching the final approach course or fix, the pilot may either complete the instrument approach in accordance with a procedure approved for the facility or continue a surveillance or precision radar approach to a landing.

(j)Limitation on procedure turns. In the case of a radar vector to a final approach course or fix, a timed approach from a holding fix, or an approach for which the procedure specifies "No PT," no   pilot may make a procedure turn unless cleared to do so by ATC.

(k) ILS components. The basic ground components of an ILS are the localizer, glide slope, outer marker, middle marker, and, when installed for use with Category II or Category III instrument approach procedures, an inner marker. A compass locator or precision radar may be substituted for the outer or middle marker. DME, VOR, or nondirectional beacon fixes authorized in the standard instrument approach procedure or surveillance radar may be substituted for the outer marker.   Applicability of, and substitution for, the inner marker for Category II or III approaches is determined by the appropriate Part 97 approach procedure, letter of authorization, or operations specification pertinent to the operation.

Index

Order Form

Books Make Great Gifts
Send A Copy Of This Book To A
Friend Or Relative

Fax this form to: (810)363-1386
Call to order: (800)207-2245
Postal orders: Odyssey Aviation Publications
                      PO Box 785
                      Union Lake, MI   48387

Company Name: _____

Name: _____

Address: ' _____

City,State,Zip: _____

Phone Number: (___)_____

Please send _____ copies of Flying On The Gages to me @ $21.95 per copy plus $4.00 shipping and handling. Michigan residents must add 6% sales tax ($1.32) per book.

Payment by:
        _____ Check
        _____ Credit Card (___ Master Card ___Visa)
        Card Number:_____
        Name on card:_____
        Exp. date:___/___

ORDER NOW